Hope and Healing for Your Marriage

Beverly McManus, M.S., L.P.C.

PUBLISHED BY
OUR WRITTEN LIVES OF HOPE, LLC

Our Written Lives of Hope provides publishing services for authors in various educational, religious, and human service organizations.
For information, visit www.OurWrittenLives.com.

Copyright ©2017 Beverly McManus
Cover Designed by Craig Gwin
Interior Designed by Our Written Lives

Library of Congress Cataloging-in-Publication Data
Beverly McManus 1966–
Love Wins: Hope and Healing for Your Marriage

Library of Congress Control Number: 2017913988
ISBN: 978-1-942923-26-8 (paperback)

Scriptures used are from the NIV, unless otherwise stated.

Disclaimer from the Author: Within the chapters of this book, I share examples of families I am humbled to work with. They are my heroes! I have changed their names to protect their privacy. I've also changed other facts about their lives, which could identify them, to further protect them. Despite minor changes in detail, the underlying struggles and corresponding principles remain accurate.

Love Wins

I have prayed for every person that picks up this book. I have prayed over your pain, your heartbreak, your marriage and your journey to healing.

I pray you find hope and restoration within these pages. I pray your heart will find the capacity to be resilient and accept the challenge of growth. Most of all, I pray you learn that now, more than ever, *Love Wins!*

Beverly McManus

With Love & Heartfelt Appreciation

I'm so grateful for my personal heritage! My beautiful family and extended family are an incredible support system to me. You have instilled in me a love for people and provided extraordinary examples for caring, compassionate and loving relationships. Thank you for believing in me so fiercely my entire life. You have sewn values and principles in me, which continue to guide my life and my practice. Thank you for the foundation of truth you established in my heart, and the endless love you surround me with.

Thank you to my parents for your unending devotion and unconditional love. You have always been a refuge, providing peace and solace for the brokenness in many lives, including mine. Thank you for not giving up on me. Thank you for breathing life into me in times of failure and weakness. I love you so much!

To my husband, Kevin, thank you for your patience, devotion, laughter, and consistency. This book would not have been a reality without your undying support. You patiently brought me my favorite foods and milkshakes, or took Kyle golfing, so I could write. There were many times you simply listened to my heart as I struggled through the writing process. You contributed immensely to making this book happen! Thank you for your steadfastness and your belief in me! We are better together!

Kyle you are a dream! You are vivacious, noisy, fun, witty, intelligent, talented, curious, and incredibly loving! You will always be the most treasured gift God has blessed me with. God has great BIG things in store for you! Perhaps one day when you have a marriage to guard, your mom's voice will ring in your ears as you prepare to love your bride with all of your heart. I love you endlessly!

My darling sister, Shawn and her husband Hub, you're pretty spectacular! Thank you for pushing me when I was insecure about my ability to complete this project. Your support in my life is irreplaceable. Your tenacity to fight for love and a future is undeniable and inspiring!

Myles, Megan, and Wes, I love you with all my heart! Myles, we have a book to write together; let's get busy! You inspire me every day! Your triumph is a light to all who know you! I believe in you! I always have and I always will!

Megan and Wes, your new marriage is a beautiful one! The life and marriage you are building is awe-inspiring and genuinely loving. You are champions of love in my world. Continue to shine bright and love each other well.

Lacey, Kris, Kerrie, and Jason, I am in awe of the love and regard you give me! Blended families prove that brokenness does not triumph!

To my devoted and loyal friends, you are my heroes! You are so supportive and you cheer me faithfully! Your belief in me gave me courage to tackle my dream! I am forever thankful for each of you!

Special Acknowledgments

I am indebted to every family and individual I have had the opportunity to work with. You are courageous and tenacious! I admire your perseverance! With every session, you make an imprint on my heart. Thank you for allowing me to be part of your journey to healing.

I appreciate Gary Nelson's family supporting my desire to share our story in the hope that others will be strengthened by it. I love each of you!

Many people have contributed to the success of this book project, and given me direction, advice, and guidance. To those listed below and all the other contributors behind the scenes, my heart is full of gratitude.

Thank you to Lindsey Hartz for guiding my *Love Wins* book launch. You are so talented and knowledgeable! I have benefited immensely from your influence on this project.

Nicole Edwards, your input and wisdom in this process is irreplaceable and invaluable to me. Thank you so much!

Craig Gwin, you are a graphic genius! Thank you for your patience with me and effectively capturing my vision for this endeavor!

Rachael Hartman, I am amazed how God lead us to one another; you are a God-send and such a blessing to me. Your passion is contagious! Thank you for publishing my work and believing in me.

Contents

1: Finding Purpose in Pain _____ 11

2: Unexpected Storms _____ 19

3: For Better or For Worse _____ 29

4: Marriage in Distress _____ 37

5: Broken Theories _____ 47

6: Attachment & Isolation _____ 53

7: Approaching Conflict _____ 63

8: Resolving Conflict _____ 71

9: Communicating Love _____ 81

10: Kindness _____ 91

11: Perseverance _____ 99

12: Forgiveness _____ 107

13: Pursue & Recover It All! _____ 115

14: A Beacon of Hope _____ 123

CHAPTER 1

Finding Purpose in Pain

The battle of life is, in most cases, fought uphill; and to win it without a struggle were perhaps to win it without honor. If there were no difficulties there would be no success; if there were nothing to struggle for, there would be nothing to be achieved.
Samuel Smiles

When I begin working with a new client, I always start the session by asking them questions to help me understand their perspective. Knowing their background helps me to figure out why they view life the way they do. Before I begin sharing the relational principals I've learned through my life and practice, I want you to understand my perspective. I will share my story in this chapter. Welcome to my worldview.

I had a simple childhood filled with a lot of love and incredible examples of how to love Jesus and people. When I was 7-years-old, my dad received God's call to serve in ministry. Most of my uncles, aunts, and cousins are pastors, missionaries, music ministers, Sunday school teachers, and evangelists—you get the point. Loving, caring, and praying for people in pain has always been a major theme in my life.

My dad evangelized for several years of my childhood. My sister Shawn and I home schooled as we traveled with our parents across the United States ministering to both children and adults. Dad preached while mom played the organ and sang with my sister and me.

A 32-foot trailer did not give us enough space to be materialistic. Some days, that motorhome seemed incredibly small, but it was home. My sister and I were always close, which was a good thing because we were always together. If the church we were ministering at had a private school, we felt as if we were in heaven and immersed ourselves in activities with the other children.

Our family ministered in hundreds of churches. We saw thousands of people begin their walk with God. At a young age, my sister and I witnessed God's miracles. I am forever grateful to have grown up in my family.

As a child, I did a lot of listening to people and studying body language. I listened for hours as my parents ministered to individuals and couples. I heard people share their pain and despair. Even as a child, I began to see that many couples struggle, carrying heavy burdens they were never meant to bear. Exposure to their stories taught me what it was like to feel hopeless, but it also planted a seed within me to find a way to bring hope to people who were hurting.

When I was a junior in high school, my dad began pastoring a church in Nashville, Tennessee. My sister, Shawn, and I had crushes on the boys who attended Christian school with us. Much to our chagrin, our parents had strict curfews and did not allow us to date. Once we were old enough to date, our parents expected the young men we dated to treat us with respect, to respect our parents and their rules, and to be full of integrity with a heart for God.

Finally, a young man I liked asked me to go to a concert with him. I was excited beyond belief. I remember dressing up and feeling beautiful. I nervously watched the clock as it approached 4:30 p.m., the time he was supposed to pick me up. Then I watched the clock tick past 5 p.m., and past 5:15 p.m.

At last the young man arrived, but instead of coming to the door, he blew his car horn signaling for me to come out to his car. His behavior did not sit well with my dad, and he told me I was no longer going on the date. After the teenage boy honked the horn a few more times, he came up to the door in a huff. My dad met him at the door and informed him the date was canceled.

To put it lightly, I was disappointed. I remember shedding tears of frustration and sadness because I had so looked forward to the evening. But something more important than a date happened that night. I learned the level of respect I deserved and began to understand how a young man who wanted to date me should treat me.

I graduated high school, went to college, and started seriously dating Gary Nelson, my high school sweetheart. He pretty much "had me at hello." He was charming, athletic, and had the most beautiful blue eyes I had ever seen. He was tall, with a gorgeous smile, and captivated my heart. We laughed a lot, dreamed together, and ministered together. We were head over heels in love. When I was 24-years-old, we had a large, romantic wedding, and said our vows with all our hearts.

We quickly settled into a beautiful life together. Gary served as the youth pastor at the church my dad pastored. We traveled a lot, had close friends and family, and were in a good place. God used Gary to speak into the lives of young people across the state. We had big dreams for our future. We hoped to be parents to at least two children and to build a home. We were well on our way toward our dreams. Gary was kind to me, and he openly expressed his love and devotion to me daily.

After about three years of wedded bliss, the enemy sought to destroy our joy and take away the glory our marriage brought to God. I am still not sure where the train derailed, but I gradually noticed a shift in my once devoted husband. He was distracted. Our marriage was not the priority it once was. He stopped attending church with me, which was a special time we cherished.

Something did not feel right. I began to ask questions. He blamed his behavior on the stress of his new job. I totally understood. He started a new position as manager at a bustling retail store. It was a demanding job; he took his work seriously and was a responsible employee. For several months, I accepted his explanation for why we seemed out-of-sync. I temporarily took over his responsibilities as the youth pastor because he was too overwhelmed at work. Shortly after that time, the truth began to expose itself. I learned our finances were in shambles and the money we had saved for our new house was gone.

My heart was breaking and nothing made sense to me. In the midst of this uncertainty, I pulled into the driveway of our home and saw a man carrying a file and taking pictures of our home.

"Excuse me, sir, can I help you?" I asked.

"I'm here to take pictures for the foreclosure," he replied.

I assured him that he was at the wrong house. He opened his file and showed me proof that our home was indeed under foreclosure. I was devastated.

Something was desperately wrong. I felt sick to my stomach. In addition to the devastating news of the foreclosure, I noticed some of our valuables were missing. If you are familiar with addiction, you likely already noticed the tell-tale signs happening in my life, which took me months to recognize. I later learned my husband had pawned off those items to pay for his addiction.

As I began probing for answers, I learned the worst possible news; my once loving and dedicated husband had a $300-a-day cocaine habit! It was a reality I refused to accept. In turn, I became the perfect enabler. I refused to let his addiction destroy our marriage. I believed that as Christians in ministry we could win this battle. My faith was strong, and I believed God would heal and restore our marriage.

My husband assured me we would be okay. We went to counseling, but he withheld the truth about his addiction. And I protected him. I did not tell anyone what was happening in our marriage. I felt it should stay between God and us. I prayed diligently, but it seemed the more I prayed, the further Gary drifted from God, and from me.

My family began to notice something was desperately wrong. They began to pray for us earnestly, and finally, my dad asked me to meet with him. I claimed to be too busy—knowing that if I started talking to my dad, the truth would come out. I wanted to triumph over the problems ourselves.

Eventually, I ran out of excuses and met my dad for lunch. It was one of the most emotional and candid moments of my life. I poured out eleven months of hidden rejection, pain, sorrow, anguish, and brokenness. I remember feeling the massive weight lift off me as I spoke truth to my father.

My dad was shattered to learn about the state of our marriage. He loved Gary like a son. Furthermore, my dad trusted Gary, giving him my hand in marriage and entrusting him to lead the youth group at the church.

The next few months were a nightmare.

Gary stayed out all night. I cried myself to sleep every night, begging God to change his heart. I grew accustomed to sleeping alone. Gary made many promises and broke them all. The intensity of emotion in our home was palpable.

I was desperate for him to be honest with me. I was desperate for him to change. The tension in the air was an easy excuse for him to be angry with me. His anger turned physical. Now, I was not only heartbroken, but also bearing physical scars of addiction, brokenness, and sin.

Throughout it all, I became a skilled investigator. I searched for clues and gathered facts, always hoping I'd find a way back to Gary's heart. I learned where he partied and who he was with. I often drove by the white Victorian rundown house that I heard was a popular drug hangout.

I remember praying Gary's car would not be there, and how I felt my stomach drop every time I saw his car parked outside of the home. One night, instead of just driving by, I decided to take matters into my own hands. Shaking like a leaf, I walked up onto the porch of the house.

I looked around and noticed the peeling paint and tattered pillars. Music blasted from inside, and people were staggering out the front door and onto the wooden porch. My heart felt as though it was going to beat through my chest. I wanted to run back to my car, but I resisted the urge and knocked. A beautiful blonde girl with glazed eyes, white short shorts, and blue tank top opened the door.

She put her hands on her hips and said, "Girl, I think you are at the wrong house!"

I told her I was looking for my husband.

She said, "I don't think you will find anyone that is husband material in this house."

"His name is Gary!" I exclaimed before she could shut the door.

"Nelson?"

"Yes! I need to talk to him!"

She looked at me shocked and replied, "I reckon you do!"

As she returned inside to search for Gary, I fought back the bitter tears burning my eyes. I peeked inside the house.

The room was hazy, and the smell of smoke filled the air. I surveyed the foreign surroundings in disbelief, and then, there he was. The man my heart adored, the man who vowed to always love and honor me, stood before me.

His eyes were hauntingly empty—completely void of the love that was once there. I felt nothing but rejection. I knew I did not belong at that house. I knew he did not want me there.

I do not remember the words exchanged in those life-changing moments. My intention was to take him home; however, it was evident he wasn't interested in leaving. As we stood in the foyer of that house, I realized the path he was choosing didn't include me.

I have no idea how I made it home safely that night. I left a piece of my heart in that house. Even after that painfully difficult night, I still held onto hope that he would come back to the happy life we once shared.

After months of waiting and fervently praying for change, I finally reached my last straw. missing for several nights. I checked the house where I usually found him, but he was not there. I was scared. I called every hospital in town to see if he was admitted to the emergency room. It took about an hour to call all the hospitals in the Nashville area. After I called them all, I started calling them again, desperate for answers.

I wanted to hear Gary was safe and alive. I repeated the cycle for hours until I physically could not do it any longer. This had become a frequent ritual for me.

After five days of anguish and despair, I was physically and emotionally exhausted. I decided to change the credit card information, so Gary could no longer access our credit.

I laid on the cold linoleum floor all night in the fetal position believing my life was over. Life without Gary seemed impossible, but I also could not continue living like this. That night, I finally accepted the fact that Gary and I would not grow old together. I finally accepted the truth that my husband was no longer the man I married. Rejection overwhelmed me.

In the weeks following, more details emerged regarding Gary's betrayals, infidelity, and lies. I withdrew from life and lost hope. The anguish I felt was unbearable. I could not believe the state of my life!

What was wrong with me? Where did I miss God's will? It was a very dark time in my life. But even in the midst of all of my brokenness, God whispered strength into me and restored my courage. I was ready to be obedient to His voice. He kept telling me that where I was, was not the end. I still loved Gary the day we divorced, but my love was not reciprocated, and I could not rescue our marriage.

After our divorce finalized, I went back to school. Initially, I did not know what I wanted to study or why I was there. I ended up choosing psychology to understand addiction better. During the next eight years, I began to learn God's plan for my pain was to help others. Thankfully, God took my brokenness and rebuilt my life in a way I could never have imagined! I am so thankful for the mercy He extended in my grief.

While I was at school, Gary's life continued to crumble. We kept in touch occasionally, but it never became any easier to watch the erosion of such a phenomenal man. Much too early, he died at 42-years-old. When he died, my anger returned. I was mad that he did not love himself enough to live out his full potential. I was angry that we didn't live out our dreams.

In the end, I have peace knowing that he had several days before his death to make his heart right with God. I am so thankful for that! God was so merciful to give him that gift and allow him to surrender to Him again before He took him home. Our God is full of grace! My relationship with Gary's family remains one of love and acceptance. They will always be family to me.

I made many mistakes during those years of crisis. I isolated myself. For over a year, I was not honest with anyone about our private marital struggle. My silence deprived Gary the opportunity to be accountable to our leaders and closest friends.

It also made me the perfect enabler. I protected Gary and rode the waves of addiction with him, instead of reaching outside of our marriage for help. Even when we did go to counseling, Gary was not honest, and I still protected him—that was a mistake. He didn't need my protection. He needed the addiction exposed so he could be honest and receive the help he so desperately needed.

So, now you know my story. You know why I am passionate to help couples find hope even in the most difficult circumstances. I want you to have hope that when you surrender your will to God's will, you can discover a renewed desire to serve Him and your spouse with fervor!

Instead of being blinded by your pain, trust that your pain is shaping you. Pain has a way of chipping away unnecessary distractions and allows you to refocus your energy, to grow, and to heal. I pray as you heal God would reveal the abundance of joy He has for you. His love will take you beyond your pain and circumstances to a bright future.

So, as the Holy Spirit says: Today if you hear His voice,
do not harden your hearts as you did in the rebellion
during the time of testing in the wilderness.
Hebrews 3:7-8

CHAPTER 2
Unexpected Storms

We want each of you to show this same diligence
to the very end, so that what you hope
for may be fully realized.
Hebrews 6:11

Six years after my divorce, I fell in love with and married Kevin T. McManus. He is a Christian music producer and builds sound and video systems for churches all across the nation. We have a loving marriage. My husband is a man of integrity. He is kind, laid back, and loving. I am sentimental, passionate, and devoted. What we have is a good thing, but we have endured our share of storms.

When we married, Kevin already had two children. Peacefully blending families can be a challenge. I call it our "fusion family." Bringing two families together requires the intermingling of personalities, hopes, and wishes. Kevin's teen children understandably experienced a lot of raw emotions when we married. Marriage brings together entire families with schedules, needs, history, emotions, insecurities and discipline styles. Merging life and finding a way to offer security, support, and acceptance in the midst of all of those changes can be difficult.

We have learned to forgive often, love more, and make a lot of sacrifices. We have found that loving each other through difficulties is paramount. His children, their spouses, and five grandchildren are all a huge part of our lives. We very much enjoy spending special occasions and holidays together.

Three years into our marriage began the beginning of several years of infertility, which drained us emotionally as individuals and as a couple. Following years of infertility treatments, at last, I conceived! It was a beautiful season of celebrating the new life we had prayed for. Our family and friends were all excited for us.

We were full of joy! Although we had not named her, I always envisioned Victoria being part of her name. We began planning her nursery, picking out furniture and choosing colors. We were so excited about the incredible gift of life God gave us!

Sadly, early in the second trimester, we received devastating news. During a routine checkup, the nurse became somber. She told us she couldn't find a heartbeat.

Kevin and I were heartbroken by the loss of our baby girl. It is a grief we still carry daily. We had many dreams for her. Our hearts were full of love for her. I isolated myself during the early stages of my grief, disappointment, and heartache.

At 39 years old, I felt that our baby girl was my last opportunity for motherhood. I was disheartened and believed I may never have the opportunity to enjoy the role of motherhood. I immersed myself in prayer, seeking God for strength and understanding.

While we were still raw from the loss of our baby, God brought the most incredible miracle into our lives—Kyle. Our baby girl's due date was January 29, 2006. Kyle was born January 3, 2006.

While we were grieving the loss of our sweet angel girl, God was preparing our gift of life! He was actively restoring our joy in the midst of our pain, but we had no idea. We had no knowledge His plan was so much bigger than what we were currently experiencing.

God was about to interrupt our darkness with fireworks! Kyle was eight-months-old when we brought him home. He is a vivacious, fun, brilliant, hilarious, and talented redhead! He turned our world upside down with his energy and love. The adoption was finalized within a week of his first birthday.

His energy, talent, and adventurous spirit fill our lives and our hearts with more laughter than we ever could have ever imagined. God gave us more than we even knew to ask for! Kyle is currently in his pre-teen years, and we are ready for all the fun that is sure to come!

When Kyle was five years old, my husband became very ill and underwent testing. We went to San Antonio to visit my sister and her family for Labor Day weekend. On the trip, my husband received a phone call. On the other end of the line was one of our doctors from Vanderbilt Hospital. My husband spoke with him for a moment, and I immediately knew the news was not good.

As soon as he hung up the phone, he began sharing the conversation with us. The bottom line was a pancreatic cancer diagnosis! He would have to visit a surgeon soon to determine a treatment plan.

I felt as if all the air drained from my lungs. I barely had the capacity to speak, but I knew I needed to say something. Finally, I said, "We will trust God to do what we are not capable of doing."

Then, I ran upstairs and buried my head in a pillow and sobbed!

After that, I did what many of us modern tech-savvy people do when confronted with the unknown. I went to my sister's office, sat at her computer and looked up pancreatic cancer and survival rates. What I found was devastating. The survival rate at five years after diagnosis was 0.02 percent.

Despite what I read, we determined early on to place our faith in God to restore Kevin's health and to provide direction for his care. By the time we went for his appointments, our faith bolstered! We literally had friends around the world praying for him. Those prayers undergirded us with faith and confidence for the journey.

The first step in Kevin's treatment plan was a procedure called the Whipple. It was a radical surgery. They removed half of his pancreas, half of his stomach, his gallbladder, and part of his intestine.

During his hospital stays, I continued my counseling practice. I spent my nights at the hospital, went to work during the day, went back to the hospital, raced home to tuck Kyle in bed, and went back to the hospital to spend the night.

My mom and sister took turns moving into our home and managing the house for me. Kyle was struggling not having his family together under one roof. He had other family members caring for him he loved and trusted, but he was confused by it all.

The hospital floor Kevin's room was on did not allow children. At one point, Kevin stayed at the hospital an entire eight weeks.

We were all exhausted with the distance, missing our routine and normalcy.

Once Kevin recovered from the grueling surgery he started a year of chemotherapy treatments. I wish I could say we were steadfast in our faith while facing that intense storm, but there were days and even weeks when we were weak. Personally, I was physically, mentally, and spiritually exhausted, and felt very isolated from my husband. All of his energy was going where it should go—toward fighting for his life. For months, I was making the major decisions we usually made together. We felt distant and out of sync.

In addition to the emotional and physical drain, we had financial pressure. Being we were both self-employed, our insurance was inadequate. My husband's medical journey to healing cost well over a million dollars and insurance didn't come close to covering the expenses.

Thankfully, my husband is a courageous fighter, and he won his battle with pancreatic cancer! God blessed our family with a miracle, one we are forever grateful for!

Although we directed our energy differently, Kevin and I fought the same battle. We understood that every effort we made ultimately made us stronger. In our most tumultuous times, we anchored our hearts in Jesus. God, our source of strength, provided solace and peace. Walking through that difficult time etched our hearts with confidence and helped us brace our relationship with comfort and strength that only God can give.

Cancer tested our resilience as a family, strained our faith, and tried to burn out our devotion, yet we emerged as a couple who gave God glory for our journey and the miracle of life. God amazingly brought my husband through a disease that over 98 percent of patients succumb to.

We knew Kevin's life was a miracle. When we finally won the battle over cancer, we began to approach life with new tenacity, determined to make the very most out of it. We were happy, thankful, and eager to resume our normal life.

Unfortunately, life never really went back to "normal." It changed. We still loved each other. We served in ministry together. We laughed together, and we spent time together, but we were not connecting like we had in the past.

It took a while for us to put the puzzle pieces together. With the help of input from his physicians, we determined that some of the losses in our relationship stemmed from Kevin's medical treatment. A condition dubbed "Chemo Brain" invaded our marriage and our relationship suffered because of it.

Chemo Brain is a cognitive impairment induced by chemotherapy treatments. It causes changes in personality, lapses in memory, and can change how a person interacts. The relationships closest to the patient suffer the most loss.

Even as I write this book, we are still struggling to make sense of our marriage and our lives. Every day it seems we face a new set of challenges. We wake up committed to face challenges together, committed to our vows, steadfast in our belief in each other, and determined to connect with each other, and grow our relationship.

Our journey to this place in our relationship has included a lot of difficult moments. There were days we felt disillusioned, scared, unsure, incapable, and frustrated. There were days we sobbed and cried out to God for the strength to stand.

I have even questioned my ability to write a book on marriage due to the storms in our lives, but it is because of the storms I am more determined than ever to provide tools to couples who are searching for answers to find ways to remain committed.

A Ring and a Promise

At some point in every marriage, it becomes a clear challenge to keep the vows to love, honor, and respect. With all the planning that goes into making a magical wedding day, sometimes the excitement clouds the realities of marriage. A flourishing marriage demands focus, determination, and flexibility. As a marriage endures stress, the glitz of the glamorous wedding day drifts into a distant memory. The effort that goes into a wedding celebration does nothing to ensure commitment of the vows.

> *When a man makes a vow to the Lord or takes an oath to obligate himself by a pledge, he must not break his word; he must do everything he said.*
> Numbers 30:2

Every marriage goes through seasons where there are no butterflies, the texts are not gushy, and there is no passionate intimacy. Marriages may face debt, loss, a diagnosis, parenting dilemmas, exhaustion, emotional pain, or betrayal. If one individual is weak or suffering, it can put a strain on their partner, and burn out both of their energy levels.

In trying times, determine to believe in your marriage, commit to giving it your very best. During tough times, you must put your commitment into action. Your marriage will not always be glamorous or resemble a fairytale. It won't have the makings of a Hollywood movie, but it will be rewarding, and God will give you the strength to live out your commitment.

Winning at Love

Nothing is predictable about marriage. You go into marriage with the very best intentions, believing in your heart that you are equipped to make your spouse incredibly happy. But nothing prepares your heart for the things you will face.

Like me, you may face illness, loss, family problems, legal problems, betrayal, and disappointments—none of which you are prepared for. No problem comes with a full disclosure of the possible effects on your marriage.

None of us can escape problems; they roll in like tidal waves. The uncertainty in the wake of life events can lead to isolation and withdrawal from what was once a nurturing, connected, healthy marriage.

One couple who came to me for counseling is a great example of how each person has no idea what they are going to face after saying "I do."

"Kathy" and "Brian" were both in professional careers when they had a baby, and were overjoyed to be new parents. Kathy took maternity leave to adjust to motherhood, but once her leave was over, she went right back to work.

The problem was that their beautiful baby boy wasn't sleeping at night. Kathy would stay up all night trying everything she could to help the baby calm and rest. At the same time, she was back to working an intense and demanding job. She was tired. Actually, she was exhausted. This schedule had been ongoing for three long years.

Her personality began changing, and Kathy started becoming paranoid. Life as they knew it unraveled. She lost her job because of her inability to maintain focus and function in her position. By the time the couple came to me, Kathy was experiencing hallucinations and psychosis.

Brian was scared but patient through our process of looking for answers. Kathy was not patient. She didn't understand the tests I ordered to rule out medical issues. She became frustrated during the helping process. She didn't trust any of the tests and felt that Brian and I were trying to control her, or insert something in her brain. In full paranoia mode, she trusted no one!

The stress level in their family was extremely high, but we were eventually able to work with other doctors to address the paranoia and hallucinations to reduce some of the stress. Her diagnosis was schizophrenia. Even with medical support, Kathy was not capable of resuming work. She was barely able to maintain their home. She was experiencing life in a different way than she previously had, and so was Brian.

Counseling helped Brian adjust his expectations for their marriage. They were able to redefine roles and adjust doing life together, but that required a lot of change through unexpected circumstances. Eventually, Kathy could focus on the tasks she needed to do daily. She also learned to manage her thoughts better which helped her attitude.

It was not the marriage either of them envisioned. It was not at all predictable, and, to be perfectly honest, it may not have been a blissfully happy marriage. But it was the marriage they were called and committed to. Kathy and Brian were determined to honor God, their commitment, and their children. They chose to respect one another and their vows. God honored their commitment by restoring joy and peace into their lives.

Love Wins

Flexibility is essential in marriage. Showing respect and kindness during difficult situations is arduous, but also necessary. You must remember the big picture of your life and your commitment to each other.

Every choice you make will either build or destroy your marriage relationship. Every decision, tone, remark, action, lack of action, and insinuation impacts the relationship and contributes to its success or failure.

Marriage can only grow and thrive if each spouse is contributing. A spouse cannot give to the relationship what they are not equipped to give. If one person has emotional damage from their past or upbringing, a previous abandonment or rejection, an addiction, or unhealthy relationship patterns, that individual must heal before beginning a new relationship or marriage.

If a wounded person has not properly healed, they will drag their pain into marriage, and their relationship will not grow beyond the pain. If a relationship is stuck, emotional wounds or damage could be the problem. Each partner must be introspective and determine the cause of the pain that blocks them from freely loving each other.

It may be helpful to consult a counselor for help resolving the deep pockets of pain so the relationship can move forward more healthily. Pain causes you to forget you are a team. But pain is never wasted. Every tear you have cried, every moment of brokenness, every time you felt rejected or betrayed, God was doing work behind the scenes. God uses pain to bring your heart and your spouse's heart to a place of surrender. He will redeem your pain, and you will impact others with your story of triumph!

Do not let any unwholesome talk come out of your mouths, but only what is helpful for building others up according to their needs, that it may benefit those who listen. And not grieve the Holy Spirit of God, with whom you were sealed for the day of redemption. Get rid of all bitterness, rage and anger, brawling and slander, along with every form of malice. Be kind and compassionate to one another, forgiving each other, just as in Christ God forgave you.
Ephesians 4:29-32

Love Wins Exercise

Examine both your individual life and your marriage. What unexpected storms are you and your spouse facing? What storms have you weathered and survived?

Are you experiencing emotional pain that is blocking your ability to love properly? Make a note of the areas in your life that need healing and open your heart to face the issues so you can bravely move forward.

Take heart—there is always hope! Put your trust in God and His plan for your life and marriage. He loves you and is with you throughout your process.

*Be completely humble and gentle, be patient,
bearing with one another in love.
Make every effort to keep the unity
of the Spirit through the bond of peace.*
Ephesians 4:2-3

CHAPTER 3
For Better or For Worse

Even the darkest hour only has sixty minutes.
Rev. C. E. Forbush

Do you remember the first few dates with your spouse? The sun seemed to shine brighter and you found yourself smiling on your drive to work. You showed them the best of you and always wanted to make them happy. You lived to build your relationship of love and adoration and your partner loved and adored in return.

Every moment was filled with thoughts of when you would see them again, kiss them again, feel their embrace again. You could talk for hours and still have so much to say at the end of the conversation. You felt loved, nurtured, and respected.

But perhaps somewhere along the way, things began to change. What happened to the blissful relationship you once had? *Reality!*

When your marriage faces unanticipated difficulties, it is easy to become disenchanted. Maybe you miss the attention your spouse once showered you with. Or maybe you are disappointed by your spouses' lack of loyalty. Your spouse may have betrayed your trust by having an emotional or sexual affair. There may be deceit in your marriage. There may even be emotional or physical abuse.

The list of potential disappointments is endless. Whatever the disappointment, every marriage experiences pain, and your reaction to that pain may be an attempt to protect yourself from further injury. When you pull away emotionally, you begin to form opinions about your spouse that are detrimental to the health of the relationship.

Winning at Love

The thing about vows, promises, covenants, and pledges is that we make them for the difficult times. A promise of fidelity is useless if there is no temptation. A vow to remain committed in bad times is not necessary if every day is paradise. Your wedding vows were not meant just for blissful days of leisurely walking on the beach without a care in the world. It is effortless to stay committed to vows on the beautiful days, and the days when you laugh hysterically at each other's jokes, reveling in the companionship of your marriage. But vows weren't made for those days; vows and covenants were made to keep us committed on difficult days.

> *Honoring your marriage commitment is about making the decision to do the right thing. It is an opportunity to be faithful to your spouse and to God by honoring your vow.*

Vows are not about the other person. They are about your heart and your response, how you react, and how committed you are. Vows are about how unbendable you are when it comes to finding hope for your marriage, and how determined you are to heal the brokenness in your relationship. Your sincerity in taking a vow will determine the actions you will take to live out what you committed to.

Vows are not conditional. Have you ever been to a wedding where in the middle of the vows they have disclaimers? "For richer or poorer, as long as poorer doesn't mean you lose your job and I have to solely support our family! I vow to be faithful in sickness and in health, as long as the sickness isn't an ongoing sickness that impairs you physically or mentally for more than two weeks!" *No!* Vows are sacred and unconditional, with no disclaimers!

The vows you take are about your devotion to this relationship that has been a blessing to your life. The vows you take are a pledge to behave and react from that day forward in such a way that your marriage is preserved, protected, and pursued. You don't make a covenant to "love, honor, and respect as long as you have an amazing career, laugh at all of my jokes, treat me like royalty daily and let me sleep in on Saturdays." We promise to forsake all others and love, honor, and respect – without conditions. Vows are resolute. They are not amendable and you took those vows knowing that the future is not predictable.

One couple in the Bible that experienced difficulty is Hannah and Elkanah. Hannah is identified as a woman consumed by prayers of desperation to birth a child. She was barren and heartbroken over the situation

1 Samuel 1:6-8 Because Hannah was unable to bear a child, her rival kept provoking her to irritate her. This went on year after year. Whenever Hannah went to the house of the Lord, her rival exasperated her until she wept and would not eat. Her husband Elkanah would say to her, "Hannah, why are you weeping? Why don't you eat? Why are you downhearted? Don't I mean more to you than ten sons?"

Hannah was not only in despair because she wanted a child, but she was being taunted by her heartless rival. Elkanah was steadfast by her side. He wanted her to eat. He wanted her to feel better. He tried reasoning with her. She was emotional, so his logical response probably did not resonate with her. Elkanah must have felt inadequate. He could not provide a solution to the problem. He hated seeing her so sad and broken. Hannah was distraught. She could not be consoled.

Hannah displayed grace under fire when she did not respond to her rival's jeers. She kept her thoughts to herself and ran to her source of strength. She made her petitions known to God. She sobbed and prayed in desperation for answers.

1 Samuel 6:17-20 Eli answered, "Go in peace, and may the God of Israel grant you what you have asked of him." She said, "May your servant find favor in your eyes." Then she went her way and ate something, and her face was no longer downcast. Early the next morning they arose and worshiped before the Lord and then went back to their home at Ramah. Elkanah made love to his wife Hannah, and the Lord remembered her. Consequently, in the course of time Hannah became pregnant and gave birth to a son. She named him Samuel, saying, "Because I asked the Lord for him."

Hannah and Elkanah stayed true to one another during very stressful times in their marriage. Their steadfastness and faithfulness were honored! Samuel was born and just as she vowed, Hannah dedicated him back to the Lord. Because of their faithfulness Hannah and Elkanah were blessed with five more children! They had three additional sons and two daughters. Samuel was one of the most important leaders in the Bible! Because of Hannah's fervent prayers, she gave birth to a son who would become a great prophet and judge over Israel.

*Let us not become weary in doing good,
for at the proper time we will reap a harvest if we do not give up.*
Galatians 6:9

Commit to the Lord whatever you do, and he will establish your plans.
Proverbs 16:3

Ultimately your marriage is intended to be a refuge from crisis and turmoil. When a storm is deep within a marriage, it disrupts your security. Tumultuous times also give the enemy easy access to target the weak areas in your marriage. Storms make your marriage vulnerable. It is vital to anchor your mind in the Bible, know where your strength comes from, pray for your spouse, and believe in your spouse.

In dark moments of distance and desperation, it is essential to have faith and confidence in each other. Believe your spouse is doing his or her very best to be the person you need them to be. Work diligently to be the person they need as well.

Finding Healing

Couples come into my office to find healing. They want their marriage restored, but occasionally it is clear they are not committed to the heart-work it takes to achieve healing. Are you committed to begin the heart-work (and it is hard work) to achieve growth and healing in your marriage?

Reconciliation is a beautiful word, with amazing end-results that requires a lot of work to achieve. Some couples panic at the thought of exposing their battered, broken, sad hearts to risk more potential harm. The thought that they may face more rejection or betrayal can be paralyzing. They are so determined to avoid vulnerability, instead of working to restore joy to their marriage, that they work harder to protect their hearts from pain. They avoid forgiveness, and unforgiveness becomes an acid, destroying the vessel that holds it.

But, as I have said before, there is hope! Even marriages that have gradually eroded over many years can be restored. There are critical steps each couple must take for a successful reconciliation. Both spouses must be one hundred percent committed to do the hard work necessary to restore the marriage. The journey to restoration will be demanding, grueling, and at times painful, but the results are worth it.

Restoration of a relationship takes time. You must be willing to make the time commitment to the healing process and be patient with your spouse. Just because your spouse isn't willing to reconcile today doesn't mean he or she will never consider it. Keep the faith!

I have witnessed many circumstances where a spouse asks for a divorce and declares the marriage is over, only to ask for the opportunity to reconcile just weeks later. Prayer changes hearts and circumstances!

Forgiveness isn't an easy process, but if you want your relationship to be healthy, forgiveness is imperative.

> *For if you forgive men when they sin against you, your heavenly Father will also forgive you. But if you do not forgive others their sins, your Father will not forgive your sins.*
> Matthew 6:14-15

There are no prerequisites in that verse that indicate you should wait until you feel like forgiving before you grant forgiveness, or that you should forgive when the perfect apology is given. God commands you to forgive when someone sins against you. Be willing to accept your spouse and forgive their shortcomings. Take a chance and God will give you the strength to forgive. He will heal your brokenness when you step out in faith.

Practice humility in your marriage. Humility reminds individuals that no one is without sin. Humility reminds people that the whole world needs mercy, grace, healing, and forgiveness. Humility opens the door to understanding. Proverbs 16:18 says, "Pride goes before destruction, a haughty spirit before a fall."

Pride keeps marriages from seeking counsel. Pride may convince a spouse that their stance is the correct one and there is no need to compromise or listen to their spouse's views. Pride persuades you that you do not need your spouse, you do not need healing, and that your spouse is blocking your happiness. Pride destroys.

You cannot change and grow until you are humble enough to accept the fact that you are flawed and have shortcomings that may be contributing to the state of your marriage. If you are too busy blaming your spouse for your stress, unhappiness, and problems, then you lack humility. It is so much easier to find a place of healing in your marriage when you wrap yourself in humility and allow God to reveal places in your marriage that require growth in your life.

The ability to forgive another person comes from God, not from your strength. It is not natural to be motivated to forgive someone who has broken your heart, disrespected you, or betrayed you. Your humanity will scream to the heavens about the injustice of their actions! You will want to blame, accuse, and pull away. To successfully heal, pray for a heart willing to forgive.

Seek the heart of God for forgiveness in your prayer walk. He will help you. If you desire God's path more than yours and you surrender your pain into His capable hands, you will be well on your way to healing. Forgiveness and healing is not an easy journey and it takes time, especially if the offenses were severe. Take a step toward forgiveness. Remember, the initial step is the most difficult.

Even if you and your spouse are not having frequent, huge arguments it does not necessarily mean that you're enjoying each other, protecting each other's hearts, or growing together. Your marriage may suffer from neglect, you may not protect each other's hearts, and may not be growing in love and intimacy. Most marriages do not fall apart because of big challenges, like infidelity, betrayal, or legal problems. More often, marriages unravel because of years of neglect, one spouse not feeling like a priority, or not being pursued.

Studies indicate it takes seven years of a disappointing marriage relationship before a couple reaches out for help. The exception comes when a crisis, such as an affair, begins imploding the marriage. In a fast-paced world, with so many demands on your time, it takes intentionality to focus on marriage. The easy response when your spouse needs something is to use your busyness as an excuse.

Life gets busy, of course, but neglecting your spouse's moments of need means missing opportunities to connect. Occasionally missing a moment to connect may not have a huge impact, but over time the repeated behavior becomes neglect. The outcome of neglecting the needs of your marriage is emotional distance, then isolation, which eventually creates resentment or bitterness. We can avoid the entire negative encounter by taking time to listen to each other's needs and attending to them.

If you do not make your marriage a priority, who will? You and your spouse must start putting more effort and engagement into your relationship to strengthen it. The changes you desire to see in your marriage may not happen overnight, but as you continue to nurture your marriage and make it a priority, it will transition into a loving, lasting, and committed marriage.

Love Wins Exercise

Every week, ask your spouse: "What have I done this week that made you feel loved? What have I done this week that made you feel like a priority?"

Asking these questions allows you both to think about the moments you felt connected. Your spouse feels attended to and heard. It also lets you know what efforts you are making that resonate with your spouse and make the greatest difference for them. Now that you know what efforts make the most impact on their heart, be more intentional about continuing those efforts in particular.

CHAPTER 4

Marriage in Distress

You have been a refuge for the poor, a refuge for the needy in their distress, a shelter from the storm, and a shade from the heat. For the breath of the ruthless is like a storm driving against a wall.
Isaiah 25:4

As a therapist, I meet with countless couples who are feeling misunderstood, betrayed, underappreciated, and judged within the relationship. As couples in crisis walk through my office doors, they are usually at the end of the marriage rope. Sometimes, they have already filed for divorce.

"The experience of slights and hurts at the hand of a partner is inevitable. After all, conflicts of interest routinely surface, and even ambiguous behaviors, if sufficiently scrutinized, might seem to reveal a partner's irritation, disappointment, or disinterest . . ." (Murray, Bellavia, and Rose 2003).

When a couple is experiencing problems, they are emotionally distant from each other, and stress and disgust is often palpable in the room. They come bearing pain. They come defeated, yet still searching for answers, and whether they know it or not—searching for hope.

Winning at Love

I remember working with a couple in their mid-30s who came to me in a very broken state. They were both professionals in the middle of buying their first home, and they had two children under five-years-old.

They were not sleeping in the same bed. They had multiple layers of pain, resentment, animosity, despair, disappointment, and disgust in their relationship. Their body language painted a clear picture. Their arms were crossed and each of their bodies was fixated toward me, careful to never look at one another. Their eyes looked empty and sad, shadowed with dark circles from sleepless nights.

They both looked desperate. They wanted their marriage to work. They wanted their children to live in a happy home, which neither of them experienced growing up.

Instead, the couple was repeating the exact same patterns they learned from their parents. They failed to communicate because communication invariably led to conflict. Both felt isolated, disrespected, unheard, and unloved.

As our sessions continued, we unraveled a lot of history. Both entered the marriage unsure of how to communicate love. They established an unhealthy pattern early in their relationship, which was quickly becoming destructive.

"Samantha" felt as if she was effectively communicating her feelings. She also felt her husband was responding well to her. However, she felt that "Ricky" was controlling her. He looked shocked at her statement. I pressed further to understand what made her feel he was controlling.

She explained that while she was busy in the kitchen one night, he asked her to change the thermostat. She felt it was controlling for him to ask her to do something he could easily do. She added there were other things that made her feel controlled.

Sometimes he would ask her to bathe the children so he could take a call for work. As we talked about the incidents, it was clear she was reacting with a defensive posture toward her husband.

Some of her natural reactions were ingrained in her from childhood. She grew up under harsh judgment, treated with a lack of respect, and blamed for things she did not do. She was accustomed to her parents micromanaging her life.

She lacked trust in her husband. She assumed he believed she was incapable of accomplishment without his direction. Her feelings caused her to become very defensive if he asked her to do anything.

As we worked through her insecurities and fears of not measuring up, she was able to relax and not jump to conclusions about her husband's comments or requests. She began to hear his words the way he intended them. If this couple had not reached out for help, I am certain their relationship would have continued down a rocky road and ended in destruction.

Thankfully, they wanted help and were willing to take responsibility to work on their individual problems. When they first came to my office, their marriage was tattered. Little by little, they found answers to their problems and began to find hope.

There is hope for every marriage in distress if both parties are willing to forgive, grow, and progress toward happiness in their relationship. The first step is to identify damaging behaviors.

Damaging Behaviors and Predicators of Divorce

Studying the predicators of divorce can help you understand how destructive behaviors can easily manifest. How a couple responds to the predictors when they become apparent will make or break the bond.

Dr. John Gottman is a well-known professor who published research on marital stability. He used scientific analysis and direct observation to identify four predictors of divorce: criticism, defensiveness, withdrawal, and contempt. Every couple experiences these four negative behavioral patterns in relationship, so simply experiencing the behaviors does not mean divorce is imminent. I use the following predictive behaviors as warnings of relational habits that can lead to more toxicity in marriages.

Criticism. When a spouse is emotionally unhealthy, he or she often projects dysfunction onto their partner through criticism. They may criticize their spouse's career choices, dissect their contributions to the family, or critique their parenting skills. No matter the vein their negativity takes to express itself, it comes from a place of confusion and pain inside of them. When a pattern of criticism continues over weeks, months, or even years, it causes a weight of anger and resentment in the marriage.

Criticism is a toxic behavior. The more criticism in a relationship, the more resentment develops. Ensuring communication is positive, uplifting, and free from criticism provides a safe foundation to quickly resolve conflict.

Defensiveness. It is normal to become defensive occasionally, but chronic defensiveness is a problem. Defensiveness creates a barrier to communication and resolving conflict. Sometimes defensiveness is a result of communication patterns passed down during childhood. Defensiveness may also develop when there is insecurity. A person may be defensive when they are avoiding taking responsibility for their actions, attitude or contributions to the broken state of the marriage. Being aware of the tendency to become defensive is the first step to keeping lines of communication open. Beyond that the goal is recognizing what causes you to become defensive and work on your inner dialog during those situations so your perspective shifts and you can hear your spouse's perspective without immediately shifting to a defensive posture.

Withdrawal. There are many reasons for withdrawal. I often see marriages where a spouse is withdrawn because they are in a controlling relationship and have lost their voice. When a spouse feels controlled, they eventually shut down. The other personality in the marriage has a louder, stronger and more resilient voice, so they give up.

Emotional exhaustion is another reason for withdrawal. If a person experiences verbal hurt, they learn not to invest their emotions into what they feel is a volatile relationship. An instinct to withdraw may be an effort to protect their heart.

Further, a spouse may withdraw after the pain of infidelity or betrayal. The pain of the betrayal may be so great that when they try to engage with their spouse, it triggers feelings of pain and rejection. Withdrawal may be the only way they know to manage their pain. The bottom line is that no matter what prompts the withdrawal, it has a devastating effect on the marriage.

Contempt. Contempt is another contributor to failed relationships. Contempt is unresolved anger, disgust, disregard, and disrespect all rolled up into one attitude. Contempt usually develops in a heart that perceives being continually neglected or abused. Constant disregard for a spouse's emotional welfare can result in continuous feelings of disgust and contempt toward the neglector. Healing requires both parties to unravel the pain driving them toward contempt, neglect, or emotional abuse.

The Angry Brain. Each of these predictors of divorce have a common emotional base—pain, and they often present themselves through anger. Anger is a normal and healthy God-given emotion that helps identify sources of pain and danger. It's how you impulsively react to anger that becomes a problem. Too often, couples aren't logically making a choice about their emotional response. They are just reacting to the pain of the moment.

While in a threatening situation, cortisol narrows the brain's focus to only process the immediate threat. When you are angry, you can *only* process negative emotions and respond to negative feelings. You become irrational if you don't change how you process information.

A tiny part of the brain called the amygdala is the emotional center of the brain. Everything you feel, including anger, comes from the amygdala. Anger is an alert in the brain signaling a potential threat to something of value. Anger is heightened anxiety while encountering something you cannot control.

When you are angry, you are often so focused on the negative stimuli, that it is impossible to have a successful, positive conversation that resolves pain. In the middle of conflict, betrayal or rejection, the amygdala prompts you to withdraw, yell, or cry.

Anger shows up in defensiveness, aggression, intimidation, and hostility. Cynicism breeds anger. Sarcasm is another twist of anger. Anger can destroy a sense of well-being, security, self-esteem, and self-image of the angry person. Anger can also destroy the recipient receiving the brunt of the emotional reaction.

Anger often stems from an inability to control or manage how people respond to you. In every situation, the emotional center of the brain constantly scans the environment asking the question, "Am I okay?"

Think about driving your car to work in the morning. Every time a car veers close to you, does not use their blinker, or pulls out quickly in front of you, the amygdala yells out, "I'M NOT OKAY!"

The job of the amygdala is to keep you safe. Your body sends the signal from the amygdala, to the neocortex which manages impulse control. Cortisol redirects blood flow to the muscles preparing you to flee the situation, or to fight.

The brain is amazing, complex, and resilient. As the danger passes, the amygdala breaths a sign of relief. "Oh, I am okay after all!"

In the Heat of the Moment

Responding in anger demonstrates a lack of tolerance for another's perspective. For most people, reacting with anger is easier than being honest about your feelings. If you can determine to act with compassion, empathy, and understanding, instead of anger, you will be able to navigate high-pressure, potentially explosive conversations more effectively.

Ideally, you should choose to respond out of love instead of anger. Your best intentions are often derailed by automatic reactions. It's like what happens if you touch something hot. You don't sit there for sixty seconds thinking about removing your hand from the hot surface. Instead, your reflexes cause you to automatically remove your hand.

Do you automatically default to sarcasm when your feelings are hurt? Or do you use angry tones or words when you feel unimportant or ignored? Never trust your tongue when your heart is hurting. You cause more harm to others when you are hurting and volatile. Many months and years of negative responses in a marriage create damaging default patterns.

Thoughtful responses require intentionality. You must reject the temptation to react *reflexively*, and instead intentionally choose to respond *reflectively*. You must take time to process feelings and decide how to communicate.

When you or your spouse experience anger in conflict, try to remember that anger is a mask hurt, fear, and frustration wear. Instead of reacting to the anger, react to their pain. Ask them what they fear the most right now. Ask them what they are most frustrated about. Ask them what you can do to help heal the pain they are enduring. By reacting to their pain NOT their anger, you allow your spouse to feel heard and validated, which goes a long way toward establishing constructive communication. When your spouse is acting irrationally, try to find out what mask they are wearing for their pain. By digging below their response, you refrain from responding to the intensity of their tone and words. Once you can communicate that you understand the pain they are expressing, it automatically neutralizes the intensity of their anger and gives you both the opportunity to effectively communicate.

To successfully navigate conflict, you must create a space for a logical response and choose not to react in anger. It may mean taking a break from a conversation. To avoid inciting feelings of abandonment, agree on a time to resume discussions.

During the window of time you are away from the conversation, focus on calming your emotions. Do what you need to do to cool down. Go for a run, a swim, or journal your thoughts. Changing scenery often allows you to be more introspective and empowers you to attach words to your feelings, resulting in more effective communication.

Tips To Disarm Anger

Along with taking a break to calm down, here are some tips to disarm anger.

Listen: What is your spouse really saying? Hear their pain. Try to understand their perspective.

Empathize: Put yourself in their place and consider how they are experiencing the situation.

Pay Attention: Be attentive to your spouse. Attentiveness disarms an angry response.

Respect: You don't have to agree with your spouse to respect them. Refrain from criticism and don't try to change or control them. Give them space to feel their feelings.

Foster Curiosity: Judgment ignites conflict. Instead of judging, try to be curious about their beliefs.

Out of the above tips to disarm anger, I want to highlight the importance of curiosity. Curiosity has the power to prompt positive discussions even in the middle of a sharp decline into angry, distant dialog. If you can show interest through curiosity, you communicate you care about what the other person thinks and feels, and that you respect and validate their opinions.

For example, you can use curiosity to disarm anger when you are in a political discussion with someone who has an opposing view. Listening to another person explain why they appreciate their candidate, and asking questions about their journey to choose to support that candidate may help you better understand their perspective. Most likely, the discussion will not cause you to consider choosing the candidate they support; however, you may gain a deeper appreciation for why they chose their candidate.

In the same way, you can apply curiosity to the way you manage conflict in marriage. You do not have to agree with your spouse to respect them, or to gain insight and understanding about their feelings. Listening is the loudest voice you can use in conflict. Listening is the most powerful action you can take when you want to reconcile your relationship.

Love Wins Exercise

Write your feelings down in a journal to help you process pain and gain perspective. If you have experienced a painful betrayal, you may decide to write a letter to your spouse.

In the letter, explain how you experience emotional pain. How did their betrayal affect you? What have you felt from your spouse since it happened? What efforts have they made to heal your pain?

Once you finish writing the letter, do not give it to your spouse. Instead, find a safe place to burn the letter. There is something therapeutic about burning the letter, which helps you release your pain into the atmosphere with the flames.

After writing and burning your letter, you have connected your feelings into words, formed thoughts, and let them go. What thoughts do you still feel compelled to tell your spouse? Keep these thoughts close, or write them down in an innocuous place. As we work through the rest of the book, work to develop healthy ways to communicate those views to your spouse.

CHAPTER 5
Broken Theories

If it is possible, as far as it depends on you, live at peace with everyone.
Romans 12:18

When you first married, did you think of your spouse as your hero? They swept you off your feet and accepted you, made you feel special, loved and adored. Do you remember how you described your spouse early in your relationship? You may have listed the characteristics you found endearing or told how he proposed or how devoted she was to you during a difficult time. However, when hurt interrupts joy, your perceptions change. It is common for couples to develop beliefs or theories about each other based on repeated behavioral patterns. Over time, your thoughts have likely changed. Maybe a series of circumstances altered your perception. Your theories about your partner may have started out positive, but if their behavior or attitude causes you pain, you may start to see them as a failure, inconsiderate, lazy, or selfish.

Can you imagine the effect such negative beliefs have on your relationship? The process of deterioration can start even after several happy years of marriage. A disappointment, failure, or deception can disrupt communication and destroy positive theories. At times, even a positive life transition can develop into negative theories.

Winning at Love

For example, I counseled a married couple I'll call "Tabatha" and "Aaron" a few years ago. They had a loving, affectionate relationship for ten years. Suddenly, the husband received a promotion at work. While the promotion was great news financially, they were not prepared for the longer hours his job would require. Little by little, Tabatha's resentment began to mount as felt she was no longer her husband's priority.

Aaron did not text his wife as often as he used to. He was too tired to enjoy some of the fun activities they once shared. Tabatha began to go to the symphony with friends, or go to the movies alone, feeling utterly abandoned.

When she brought up her feelings, her husband shrugged them off and became frustrated that she was not more supportive of his career. Aaron's response created an emotional tornado in Tabatha's heart! After months of reaching out and feeling rejected, she was certain her theory was correct. She was no longer a priority to her husband.

Tabatha had created and nurtured a belief, or theory, that her husband cared more about his job than her or their marriage. It did not matter whether her theory was true or not, her perception was now her reality. She collected "evidence" to prove her "case" was true.

Each time that Aaron made a decision, his wife judged him based on the theory that she was not a priority. If he forgot to bring milk home, well, of course, it was because she was not a priority. If he forgot about an appointment they had, it was because she was not a priority. She thought to herself, "If it were a work appointment, he would not forget!" If he did not return a text promptly, it was because she wasn't a priority. Many times a day, Tabatha found responses and attitudes that confirmed to her that she was not a priority.

She began to believe her false perception of reality and saw her husband as the "bad guy" who forgot his family. The truth was, he adored his wife, but was overwhelmed in his new position and needed a few months to adjust. He took on new responsibilities because his wife believed in him.

Sadly, by the time the husband found out about how abandoned Tabatha felt and her theory, in her mind it was "case closed." She was certain he was guilty of making her last in his priorities. Her outlook affected her attitude toward her husband and resulted in a downward decline. She began to respond to him out of her disappointment. She treated him with less respect. She disengaged from the marriage because she did not feel loved or supported.

Thankfully, the couple sought help in the middle of their painful spiral. Through counseling, we identified Tabatha's damaging theory about her husband and restored health to their marriage. Tabatha began to acknowledge Aaron's true thoughts toward her, and stopped "mind reading." Aaron became aware of his wife's feelings and insecurities, which resulted from his focus on work obligations.

They began to engage in positive discussions about feelings of isolation, which had progressively worsened for both. They committed to being more supportive, and agreed to openly talk about any negative feelings, thoughts, or theories. Their efforts renewed security and restored hope for the future of their marriage.

Guard your heart and your marriage against destructive theories about your spouse. Theories born out of pain and isolation will aim to destroy what is positive, kind, and resolute in your relationship. Broken theories destroy good marriages, so constantly guard against toxic negativity.

You are not a failure if your marriage has difficulties. Experiencing difficulties makes you human. Everyone goes into marriage with baggage, pain, bruises, and misconceptions, but being aware of broken theories can prevent them from destroying your relationship.

Do not be misled: Bad company corrupts good character.
1 Corinthians 15:33

Act-Don't React

Reacting to pain and believing a negative theory about your spouse is damaging. Forming negative opinions about your spouse creates room for disrespect in your relationship. Disrespect breeds broken communication, and a lack of emotional intimacy.

Unaddressed or unmanaged stress may result in overreaction. If you find yourself frequently reacting to situations in your marriage and family in an exaggerated way, it may be a good time to consider what you can do to manage stress in a healthy way. By monitoring your emotional health and stress levels, you can maintain clarity and make better decisions.

You can stop the downward emotional decline by talking about how your spouse's behavior and decisions affect you. Communication will bring peace to your heart and your relationship. Ephesians 5:11 says, "Have nothing to do with the fruitless deeds of darkness, but rather expose them." You give the enemy room to destroy your marriage when you do not communicate your concerns, hurts, and feelings with your spouse. Your unspoken feelings will grow into something you never intended.

If you continue to mentally rehearse negative theories regarding your spouse, it will taint your attitude. Your attitude can lead to a disrespectful demeanor, and your communication could reflect contempt and dishonor toward your spouse.

Many couples simply avoid issues in their relationship because they are uncertain how the communication will end. They fear their spouse's reaction and rejection. They fear conflict, isolation, or abandonment, and the fear weighs heavily on them. Imagine the pain trapped in a heart that has learned not to express feelings. Eventually, the pain turns to resentment, anger, and bitterness.

Often, a spouse will carry the weight of unresolved issues for years to "protect" the relationship. I call this the "rescuer's syndrome." While a rescuer may have good intentions, they show a lack of confidence that the relationship is strong enough to work through conflict. They want peace, and to avoid conflict, so they avoid talking about their pain. They struggle, feeling isolated, lonely, detached, abandoned, and forsaken.

Carrying pain like a prized possession, unwilling to forgive or heal, keeps a person victimized. Be cautious not to make a trophy out of your pain or relationship struggles. Be willing to let go of pain or disappointment so you and your marriage can heal.

The goal of marriage is to grow together through challenges, allowing God to guide, strengthen and heal you both individually and as a couple. Your weakness and brokenness does not limit God. Your lack of vulnerability doesn't derail God's plan for you or your marriage. Your failures do not cause Him to second guess His purpose for your life. He isn't suppressed by your doubts. You can trust Him to walk with you through the healing process!

Love Wins Exercise

It's almost impossible to hide when you're looking directly into your partner's eyes for five minutes at a time. Set a timer, sit together, make sure you're at eye level with each other, become comfortable, and softly gaze into your spouse's eyes.

The exercise will bring important emotions to the surface. Talk about what you feel. If this exercise is difficult for you, then your relationship is suffering from lack of emotional intimacy. Keep trying the exercise daily. It is a great way to check the pulse of the relationship between you and your spouse.

CHAPTER 6
Attachment & Isolation

Above all else, guard your heart, for everything you do flows from it.
Proverbs 4:23

Have you ever planted a garden and then lost interest in it? What happened? The weeds overtook the beauty of the garden. What you ended up with did not resemble what you had envisioned. To achieve a beautiful garden, you must tend to it, weed out what doesn't belong, and nurture what does belong.

Your marriage is a lot like a garden. If you ignore it, put it on auto pilot and neglect your partner's needs, it will become a mess. You need each other. You need connection. You need time. You need nurture. A successful marriage communicates well, forgives often, extends grace daily, and cares deeply.

What is Attachment?

Attachment theory is a psychological model that attempts to describe the dynamics of long-term and short-term interpersonal relationships between humans. Attachment depends on the person's ability to develop basic trust in their caregiver and their self.

In infants, attachment works as a motivational and behavioral system that directs the child to seek proximity to a familiar caregiver when they are alarmed. A child with healthy attachment has an expectation they will receive protection from their caregiver. As a child experiences patterns of reliability, comfort, and responsiveness from their parents, a bond is formed. The attachment bond gives the child assurance the parent will meet their needs.

Recent research suggests couples desire the same safety and security of an attachment bond in marriage. When a spouse is emotionally unavailable it cripples the relationship. Emotional connection is vital to the health of a marriage. A marriage void of emotional connection, has no attachment. Times of crisis and conflict reveal attachment styles and determines how couples navigate communication and relate to each other.

You undoubtedly started your relationship feeling very secure. Upon making a commitment to the relationship, you found comfort and acceptance, and began to trust your spouse. Falling in love has a lot to do with the safety we feel when we are around the person we love. Because we share a mutual bond of love, we feel accepted, and believe in the relationship.

Maintaining a robust sense of attachment is essential to the health of marriage because attached couples can trust, accept, comfort, and reassure each other. Humans long for a sense of safety and security. When we feel emotionally disconnected, we become consumed with fear and insecurity.

The more distress and hopelessness in the relationship, the more automatic and rigid the emotional and behavioral responses between partners will be. Couples who are emotionally disconnected become caught in a negative loop of reactive behaviors. Each time their partner fails to respond to their needs, a sense of panic overwhelms them and insecurity intensifies. If the cycle repeats over and over, the insecurity continues to grow and the gap between the couple widens.

Detachment typically occurs when:
- Your upbringing did not model "attached" relationships.
- The pain you experience in the relationship or in past relationships is so intense that your default reaction is detachment.
- Unresolved conflict causes you to detach because the relationship does not feel emotionally nurturing or accepting.

- Other causes of detachment include betrayal, or not feeling like a priority. Sometimes, a spouse suffers from fear of attachment. They may have had a long history of abandonment and rejection that has caused them to fear of emotional intimacy. When a spouse is emotionally detached, the relationship lacks the nurture, response, and connection necessary to flourish.

Secure attachment allows a relationship to abound in empathy and compassion. A relationship with secure attachment will also have appropriate boundaries and the couple will enjoy open, nurturing communication. A securely attached couple enjoys each other's company, relies on each other, and seeks to strengthen each other. Attached couples have honest communication and both spouses feel accepted and feel comfortable sharing their deepest feeling and most intimate thoughts.

In my nearly twenty years as a marriage counselor, I have seen many families in unavoidable crisis. Unexpected tragedy, illness, or death can devastate a family, leaving everyone in shock and trying to survive. Sometimes the most difficult, uncontrollable events bring families together. It is more common for a marital crisis to develop from <u>completely avoidable</u> reasons rather than from unexpected tragedy.

In the first book of the Bible, Genesis, God gave Eve to Adam because He did not want him to live alone. Since the beginning of creation, God's plan was companionship. God desires couples to enjoy emotional attachment. Sadly, due to sin, isolation and lack of attachment is a reality for many people even still today.

Too often, I see couples with empty eyes and broken hearts sitting across the room from me. Although they are married, they each feel very much alone. They live in a home with a spouse who is isolated, guarded, and shares little to no emotional dialogue, nurturing, or connection. I often hear couples say, "It feels like we are business partners," or, "We are merely roommates."

Isolation is a choice that devastates even the most stable marriage relationships. Often, one partner will isolate because of shame after giving in to temptation and sin. Isolation is completely avoidable, but in the middle of hurt, it is the easy way out.

The good news is, emotional attachment is also a choice. Choosing to engage rather than to isolate will bring healing to seemingly impossible situations. The following true story is a perfect example of what happens when a couple chooses to work through hurt and pain, rather than to isolate.

Winning at Love

A beautiful couple came to my counseling office during the darkest trial of their lives. "Paula" and "Sam" were married eighteen years and had three beautiful children. The couple was very close while dating and during the early years of marriage. They shared their feelings vulnerably and were intertwined in healthy emotional attachment.

They dated for three years before marrying, enjoying many adventures including parachuting, bungee jumping, and mountain climbing. They loved the fun, laughter, and the thrill of their escapades.

Four years into their marriage, Sam started a business, with Paula's full support. A lot of his focus shifted to his company as he was determined to succeed, and he did succeed. His company saw epic growth. He had a staff of over 200 employees and the business gained national recognition. The larger his corporation grew, the more energy it took to run it. He spent more and more time at the office.

Paula did not work with Sam in the family business, but she did have a presence there. She came by occasionally for a party or to go to lunch with her husband. Eventually, their lunch dates became nonexistent. As time went by, she began to feel unwelcome when she stopped by the office unannounced.

Then one day, Paula received an unsolicited voicemail warning her that Sam was in a relationship with a female employee. Paula began questioning her husband, but he denied any involvement with someone else. Paula trusted Sam and believed nothing was going on, but her fear added to her stress and the division in their marriage.

One evening, Sam came home from work and asked Paula for some time to talk. He nervously began to share the ugly truth, and it was gut wrenching. He was having an affair with one of his employees, and had been for the past seven years! But there was more. Now the woman was two months pregnant with his child.

The truth was more than Paula could process. The life she thought she had was a lie, and the fantasy was ripped from her heart. The marriage she had invested in was not what she thought it was. She was betrayed, manipulated, used, and deceived. She was angry, disgusted, bewildered, and confused.

But she was also done!

She wasn't going to stand by and allow Sam to continue cheating on her with her full knowledge. She asked him to leave. He did leave, but was desperate to save his marriage, so he called me.

Paula wanted to forgive him, but the fact that there was a living reminder of his betrayal was too much. It would no longer just be about their family. Now there was another child involved. Sam was ashamed of his decisions and completely broken. He wanted very much to save his marriage, but had no idea what to do!

His repentant attitude was helpful in softening Paula's heart. With forgiveness, emotional healing began and they came to a better place relationally by the time the baby was born.

But the baby brought new problems. The birth triggered all of Paula's negative emotions again, and it brought up new dilemmas. How would Sam navigate seeing his baby? How would he and Paula tell their children about the baby? How would they handle their children's emotions?

It was a complex set of circumstances. I worked with Paula and Sam individually, and as a couple. Eventually, I brought their children in for family counseling as well.

Paula and Sam were an incredibly courageous couple that beat the odds! They found their personal paths to recovery, healing, and hope. They consistently relied on faith in God and were willing to take the difficult steps necessary to achieve restoration.

They chose emotional attachment rather than isolation. The recovery of their marriage was a miracle! God heals and restore relationships in circumstances like Paula and Sam were in, when both people are willing to face their pain and their shame, and to choose repentance and forgiveness.

A Dangerous Tool of Isolation

In Sam's case, perhaps it was the excitement of a high-risk behavior that led him to engage in an on-going adulterous relationship. Regardless of why the relationship started, isolation was in the mix. Sam isolated part of himself from his wife, separating her from the business side of his life over time. He kept the affair secret for a very long time. As a result, he kept his heart isolated from his wife, family, and God until he brought the truth into the light.

Sexual sin is pervasive, and lends itself to secrecy and the destruction of emotional attachment. Extra-marital affairs, fornication, sexual abuse, homosexuality, and a host of other ways to act out sexual sin destroys a person's ability to attach through intimacy. Pornography is one of the most dangerous tools the enemy uses to destroy intimacy in marriage.

In this section, I focus on the problem of pornography instead of writing about sexual sin in general because of how widespread and easily accessible it is. Pornography has become a part of American culture. The devastating effects and accompanying principals concerning pornography can be applied to any sexual sin. As with all sexual sin, if you are engaged in pornography, you are unfaithful to your spouse.

Pornography is a form of betrayal, both to a marital partner and to God. God created sex for married couples as an intimate time for physical and emotional sharing and attachment. Cultivating a healthy sexual relationship creates a richer, closer, deeper emotional attachment between a husband and wife. Any sexual act outside of the marriage relationship is shallow and empty. Pornography disconnects partners, replaces physical intimacy, and destroys marriages.

The resulting pain of pornography is heart-wrenching. Many clients pour out their brokenness, explaining the abandonment they feel, and sharing their experience of betrayal after learning of a spouse's on-going porn addiction. Pornography ravages marriages and destroys the intimacy God intended for healthy relationships.

Despite how powerfully devastating it is, pornography is a choice that is completely avoidable! So many disappointments and stressors are completely out of our control, but pornography is a monster welcomed into life via technology. Just as easily as it is accessed, it can go away with the click of a button. The accessibility of pornography makes it a pervasive tool meant to destroy. When a marriage partner engages in pornography they are less responsive to their spouse, less interested in physical engagement, and are not as emotionally available.

Pornography is like a cancer that slowly grows, destroying a marriage from the inside out. It suppresses passion, abolishes trust, and destroys romance. Like all sexual sin, it may seem sensual, provocative, alluring, or captivating, but it ends in destruction. When a person engages in porn, they invite other people into the sanctuary of their private passion, a place created for pleasure between married partners.

Porn erodes intimacy, and affects the expectations for sex. When the mind is filled with seductive scenes and images, reality is less captivating, and expectation levels become unrealistic. If one partner is addicted to porn, their spouse will feel disappointed and less desirable, which leads to less healthy sex, lower self-esteem, and more engagement in pornography.

Pornography objectifies people, turning them into a cheap and disposable commodity. Men and women that watch porn subject themselves to images, violence, rape, anger, and much worse. Each exposure corrupts the viewer's perspective, resulting in demeaning and twisted beliefs.

I cannot overstate the negative impact of pornography on marriage. Patrick Fagan, Ph.D. completed a research study on how often pornography was linked to divorce. In fifty six percent of divorced couples, Fagan found one partner was obsessed with pornography. His findings show over ninety percent of men have viewed internet pornography. Pornography is so easily accessible, it is the number one temptation men face. Women are not exempt; porn addiction is also rapidly increasing in females.

The more a person engages in pornography, their appetite for it increases until it becomes an addiction. In his clinical research, Dr. Victor Cline described the progression of porn addiction as "escalation." The study showed that being married did not solve the porn addict's problem. Their addiction and escalation was due to powerful sexual imagery in their minds, implanted there by exposure to pornography.

With the passage of time, the sexual addict required rougher, more explicit, and more deviant sexual material to achieve a physical orgasm. It's like what happens with drug addicts. Over time, there is nearly always an increased need for more of the stimulant to obtain the same effect.

Scripture is clear that we all will be tempted, but God's faithfulness is our security in the moments temptation tries to overwhelm us. God will be your buffer from the trap of temptation if you make Him your source of strength.

> *No temptation has overtaken you except what is*
> *common to mankind; and God is faithful,*
> *He will not let you to be tempted beyond what you can bear.*
> 1 Corinthians 10:13

Healing from Isolation and Renewing Attachment

Before a major sin-crisis hits a marriage, one partner will often isolate. Isolation is a tell-tale sign trouble is imminent. Watch for it, and do everything you can to foster intimacy, transparency, and invade isolation with truth.

Guard your heart and your marriage against the evils that seek to destroy the strength of your relationship. Be careful what you allow into your heart, what your ears hear, and what your eyes see. What you see and hear shapes your heart and desires. You can protect and safeguard your marriage by guarding from pornography and other destructive and isolating behaviors. Affairs happen when you turn your heart away from your spouse. Make sure you treat your partner like the treasure they are to you; love them well.

Healing patterns of interaction and communication can help your marriage grow back into an attached relationship. To heal a relationship that is detached, both parties must engage in the healing process. It will require forgiveness, honest communication, prayer, and integrating Biblical knowledge.

Your brokenness is not beyond repair. God can speak life into any situation; remember Paula and Sam. But beware! The enemy is intent on destroying your marriage. Temptation is always present. Be vigilant and wise. Stay constantly focused and on-guard to protect your marriage and life from destruction.

Love Wins Exercise

Try this little exercise when you feel distant from your spouse and want to feel reconnected. Sit side by side, or lay by each other. Place your foreheads together, and take deep breaths together. Focus on matching your spouse's breathing patterns as they inhale and exhale slowly.

As you become more in sync with your breathing, you will feel an emotional shift as well. You will have created a beautiful space for sharing. After seven or more breaths in sync, share a dream, an insight, a memory or listen to your spouse's thoughts.

CHAPTER 7

Approaching Conflict

The goal of marriage is not to think alike, but to think together.
Robert C. Dodd

Every relationship experiences some level of conflict. If there is no conflict, there is either a lot of avoidance or a lot of secrets. Your approach to conflict is usually shaped by the role models you grew up watching. If one or both parents screamed during conflict, you may tend to raise your volume in an attempt to be heard during emotional discussions. If one or both parents stomped out of an argument, you may find yourself retreating when conflict arises. Handling conflict well means being intentional about the relationship and understanding the impact conversations will have on you and your spouse.

When we study children, we find that from a very young age, girls communicate with words. If you watch a three-year-old girl play, she uses words to articulate where her doll is going, how long she will be there, and who will be joining the activity.

While watching three-year-old boys play, we find they rarely use words. They use noises. As they play with cars, they use sounds such as "zoom," or "varoom."

Clearly, males become more comfortable using words, learn to articulate and do so efficiently; however, typically females use more words daily to express their feelings. Females are often very comfortable sharing their concerns, fears, and excitement regarding most any issue. Males have a predisposition to be less forthcoming. In conflict, men tend to be less willing to communicate—often because they are too overwhelmed by the emotion of the conflict.

Women frequently communicate their thoughts expressively. This is usually difficult for men to process. A woman's brain processes information, hurt, pain, and celebration through a lens of emotion. Men typically process information through a lens of logic. Perception between the sexes is very different. Their processing and communication styles are unlike one another's. Interestingly, some couples reverse communication roles.

In this chapter, we will examine how the different ways we approach conflict can determine the outcome.

Winning at Love

My husband, Kevin, and I do not often argue. When we do argue, I like to believe it is concerning something extremely significant. I trust we learn valuable lessons in the process of arguing that help us grow and provide insight to each other. The following story is an example of our communication style during conflict.

I thoroughly enjoy making sure the décor in our house is special and inviting. I like to make sure the chair in the corner is perfectly draped with a blanket, and that a pillow is placed just so. I decorate our guest rooms with care; every detail is gratifying and enjoyable for me to plan and implement.

At Christmas time, my husband decorates the front lawn with Christmas decorations. The festive decorations usually consist of clear lights lining the trees, and magnificent wreaths hung on the front windows of our home. It is simple and beautiful. I love it.

A couple of years ago, in the middle of all the recitals, concerts, and parties of the Christmas season, I remember running through the kitchen and seeing my husband with a huge, red, glittery, plastic bow in his hands. I couldn't fathom what he could possibly need the bow for, but I didn't have time to slow down and ask. The next morning, I raced out of our house. I was going to take my son to school and then head to my office for a full day of counseling sessions. As I backed out of our driveway there it was!

My husband had randomly put the enormous, hideous, red bow on the front of our home under a window. Why in the world would he hang a massive, glittery, plastic red bow under a window on the front of a house? What could he be thinking? It was awful enough he bought it to start with, but now he had fastened it to the front of our home.

I was livid! So, I did the best thing I could. I texted him. It was not a sugary, sweet, loving text. As I remember it, I commanded him to, "Take that ugly red bow down immediately!" I mentioned something about it looking like rednecks had moved into the neighborhood.

I didn't hear from him for several hours. When he finally did text me back, he was to the point. "Taken care of," he replied.

That night I decided to bring up the horrific bow at dinner.

"What in the world were you thinking?" I asked. He responded by sharing that he was just trying to make our home festive. He realized he failed to ask my opinion on the big red bow, but he thought it looked merry and joyful and thought it would be a great addition to our festive look.

Kevin's feelings were obviously hurt. He had worked diligently on the Christmas décor and felt he was contributing to our joyful season by doing so. He predicted I would appreciate his efforts. And I should have, but I didn't. Thankfully, we ended up laughing about the entire event. To this day, I am not a big fan of big red bows anywhere in our home.

We did not communicate well through that minor fiasco. I initiated the communication with a very insensitive text that gave no regard for his feelings or effort. He felt unappreciated and disrespected. Although the conflict was light-hearted, it bears the mark of patterns we easily become entrenched in. Don't be so desperate to be understood that you fail to be understanding.

Communication during Conflict

Conflict is not usually about who is right, or how wrong the other person is. Conflict is more about the search for respect, understanding, acceptance, or being heard. Having a difference of opinion does not destroy a relationship, but how you handle conflict can fragment a relationship.

Characteristically, when conflict arises, the person feeling the most pain sets a tone for the communication. The person may be angry, feel hopelessness, or overpoweringly loud. Whatever tone the hurt person sets, the other spouse inclines to respond at the same level. If a spouse is screaming, the other spouse may scream back, not because they are angry, but because one matches the tone one is spoken to in order to be heard. *It is easier to be angry than it is to be openly honest.*

To diffuse intense dialogue, one may ask questions about the other person's anger, hurt, or disappointment. Asking questions communicates to your spouse you care and want to understand their pain. Your questions can help turn the course of the conversation.

It is easy to blame the other person during a conflict. Avoiding taking responsibility usually makes blaming the next best option for defense. Blamers typically react intensely, and shift responsibility entirely to their spouse—further igniting anger and resentment.

It is important to avoid thinking negatively about your spouse, which will impair your judgment. *If you believe the worst about your spouse, you will respond defensively or aggressively during conflict. Justifying your actions and words will not solve the problem.*

Withdrawing and building walls will also intensify conflict. Focus on giving healthier responses to shift the tone and trajectory of the conversation. Responding without blame and judgment gives room to help your marriage heal.

Common Mistakes To Avoid During Conflict

During intense moments of conflict, it is difficult to pull back and consider the impact of your choices. A defensive posture is a common reaction when in a quarrel. A spouse who feels disrespected may become angry and use hostile words in self-defense. When a spouse is hurting, they might withdraw. Others may become argumentative. Still, others are so determined they are right, they fail to listen to their spouse. Many couples grow into the habit of frequently raising their voices during conflict, or making assumptions, which can escalate conflict to a destructive level.

In the Bible, the first husband, Adam, demonstrated destructive behaviors during conflict, which resulted in more damage. When God confronted him about eating the fruit from the tree of the Knowledge of Good and Evil, the first thing Adam did was cast blame on Eve and God Himself. "The woman you put here with me – she gave me some fruit from the tree, and I ate it" (Genesis 3:12). He had the nerve to blame God—a desperate alibi!

Adam failed to take responsibility or handle confrontation with ease and grace. Instead, his response reflected immaturity, pride, a lack loyalty, and a lack of respect for God and Eve. I wonder how Adam's reactions affected his marriage. I wonder how Eve responded to the blame. I would love to know how they approached conflict resolution. There was no leaving that marriage! They had to resolve their conflict.

We previously discussed gardens. Have you ever planted a garden? Maybe you planted tomatoes and they didn't grow. Did you blame the tomatoes? Or did you look for potential reasons the plant did not do well? Was there enough sun? Enough water, or too much? Did the soil need changed?

Most of us won't blame a plant for dying, but if we have problems in a relationship we may quickly blame the other person! Blaming them doesn't resolve the problem. Looking for a reason behind the problem, and then for a solution is the best approach.

Negative reactions perpetuate the cycle of pain and cause distress, leaving both spouses feeling rejected and disrespected. The longer a negative cycle exists, the more likely the couple will suffer from problems and battle with trusting each other. When trust erodes, fear steps in, which commonly results in further isolation.

By studying the following common mistakes made in marriage, you can better recognize what triggers a negative cycle in yourself or your spouse during conflict, and can change the trajectory of the conversation before it is too late.

Defensive. You become defensive when you take the conflict personally and begin to protect yourself, instead of staying vulnerable and listening to your spouses' pain.

Constant Correction. During a conflict, do you try to show your partner where they were wrong? Do you only listen to use their comments against them?

Anger. When you cannot control a conversation, you may become anxious, which often surfaces as anger.

Blame. As discussed earlier, it is easier to blame than it is to be introspective and think about how you can change.

Criticism. Perhaps you criticize to deflect the responsibility from yourself onto your spouse.

Hostility. Speaking in a hostile tone isolates your spouse and does not create a safe space to work through the conflict. Sometimes you may raise your volume out of anger, because you do not feel heard, or because you are speaking over your spouse. No matter what the reason, it is not beneficial to raise one's voice. In fact, we know from research, when someone yells, you do not hear what they are saying, you only hear their anger.

Assumption. When emotions escalate in conflict, do you make assumptions about what your spouse was trying to say or what they meant? Assumption is unfair. Allow your spouse to speak for him or herself. Ask questions if you are unclear what was intended or implied.

Disrespect. When you feel unheard, neglected, or betrayed, you will often react in a way that shows a lack of respect for your spouse.

Bringing up the past. Rehashing the past can launch a downward spiral of negativity, which is overwhelming for any conflict and both parties will begin to feel a sense of helplessness.

Minimizing. It is a common tactic to minimize what you do not understand. Lecturing, scolding or berating has no place in a positive marriage setting. For instance, if you respond to your spouse's pain with a rant like the following:

"Well, it is ridiculous to get upset about something like that! If you are going to be upset, at least let it be about something worthwhile."

Perhaps, it would be better to say you do not understand why your spouse feels the way they feel, and take responsibility for your perspective rather than haranguing them. You may think your spouse is having an outlandish overreaction, but try to empathize instead of sermonizing and lessening their apprehensions.

Love Wins Exercise

Evaluate your conflict skills. Which of the common mistakes listed above reflect your emotional reactions? Plan to change your responses into thoughtful actions that produce a positive reply from your significant other.

Frequently ask your partner: "When do you find our communication most difficult? How can I be more supportive of you?"

CHAPTER 8

Resolving Conflict

Between stimulus and response there is a space.
In that space is our power to choose our response.
In our response lies our growth and our freedom.
Victor Frankl

Victor Frankl was an Austrian neurologist and psychiatrist who suffered greatly during the Holocaust as a concentration camp survivor. He coped with the trauma by thinking of life beyond the torture. His life goal developed to help others find meaning in the midst of suffering. Frankl spent a significant portion of his life helping others find goodness and purpose in life, despite pain.

He taught what it means to be human and how to be our best in the worst circumstances, despite our inclinations to react impulsively. When we encounter conflict and circumstances that lure us toward negative reactions, we have the ability to respond positively.

Even if the situation feels hopeless, set goals about who you want to be in your marriage. If you wait until you are in the middle of a stressful moment to decide how you want to act, you may react on reflex and cause even more damage to your marriage. Envision yourself having a positive disposition in stressful situations. As you begin to imagine yourself staying calm in the midst of conflict, your emotions are more likely to follow suit.

Winning at Love

A cherished couple came to me for counseling before they were married. "Claire" came from an abusive background. Her parents were drug addicts and dealers. Her home environment was anything but nurturing. She grew up around drama, drugs, guns, and addiction. There was violence, and threats of violence, daily. Everyone in the home was abused nonstop, including the fragile baby girl, Claire.

When she was five years old, Claire's father was high on drugs and attempted to suffocate her to death; he almost succeeded. An acquaintance who happened to be in the home called 9-1-1 and Claire was rushed the hospital. They admitted her into PICU where she fought for her life for several weeks.

Both of her parents went to prison for endangering her life and attempted murder, and she was placed in foster care for several years. Foster care, while more stable, was not nurturing. She bounced around to several foster homes. The people were decent, but she never felt loved or accepted.

Despite her feelings, Claire was a determined little girl. She was smart and did well in school. She was shy and relationships were difficult for her, so most of her energy went to academics and sports—areas where she excelled. By the time I met her, Claire was engaged to a wonderful young man named "Richard."

Unlike Claire, Richard was raised in a loving, encouraging environment. His parents were married for forty-five years, and had set a great example for him. He was excited about building a loving relationship to enjoy for life. The problem was, Claire was extremely insecure and unsure how to navigate a relationship. She did not trust Richard, and was easily triggered when she felt unsafe or unprotected.

I spent several months on individual therapy with Claire. We worked on her fear of abandonment and trigger reactions to pain. We also had her treated with EMDR, a treatment that addresses PTSD trauma and minimalizes its effect on the brain and responses. Eye movement desensitization and reprocessing (EMDR) is a new, nontraditional type of psychotherapy.

While working with them as a couple, I helped Richard learn new listening skills and how to respond compassionately to Claire's fear responses. Richard felt overwhelmed by Claire's heightened response levels to incidents that seemed minimal to him, so he often reacted to her in anger. His anger made her feel even more unsafe. Her natural fear response was flight, so she would often leave their home in anger. It scared Richard to see Claire speed out of the driveway in a rage. He did not have a clue where she was going, or if she would be safe. It was exasperating for him to be left behind worrying about her safety and concerned about how their relationship would survive the turbulent outbursts.

In our combined couple work, we found ways Robert could make Claire feel secure. She needed stability and safety. If they had unexpected company, long hours at the office, or a flat tire, she immediately felt insecure, which set their relationship up for potential conflict. Richard's response to common life episodes was pivotal in helping Claire.

Claire began recognizing when she felt insecure and unloved, which helped her connect her feelings to words, so she could communicate to Richard and he could put their safety plan into action. The safety plan involved Richard assuring Claire that working late had nothing to do with his feelings for her, and that his devotion was steadfast. As soon as he arrived home, he would hug her, assure her of his love. After that, they would do something she enjoyed that would calm her heightened sense of insecurity, such as walking around the neighborhood or sitting by the pool with a cup of hot tea.

Richard loved Claire so much he was willing to make every effort necessary to address her insecurities and build a foundation to nurture her wounded heart. Claire knew the diligent hard work it took to cultivate her feelings of security, and she was appreciative of Richard's effort.

Their relational goal was to prevent insecurity with connection and reassurance. It was important for Richard to respond to Claire with connection, so she could feel a sense of security. Doing so would prevent conflict and isolation—triggers for her trauma response. It was important for Claire to be aware of her emotions and to be ready to share how she was feeling rather than run from the situation.

Both Richard and Claire grew immensely throughout the counseling process. Their love and devotion for one another deepened, and they are a shining example of how a relationship can be strengthened with a lot of work, insight, sacrifice, and love.

Although your upbringing may not have included the abuse, rejection, and betrayal Claire experienced, we all have pain and the need for belonging. Conflict can tap into pain, causing us to respond to fear instead of engaging in healthy dialog. As a couple, determine what behaviors and situations trigger a trauma response in your marriage.

Is it blaming or accusation? Is it a tone? Is it your partner's approach? Is it their lack of listening skills? Do you feel judged by them? Do you feel minimized or unheard? Once you determine your primary trigger, discuss ways you can better respond to one another and nurture listening and connecting patterns.

Don't be afraid to discuss important matters in your relationship. Instead, be afraid of avoiding the important conversations. *When you avoid talking about important matters, you are deciding to put your relationship at risk.* Have a plan for avoiding trauma triggers, be bold and use the new skills you are learning to build solid communication patterns.

Respectful communication under conflict or opposition is an essential and truly awe-inspiring ability.
Bryant McGill

You cannot fix your spouse, but that doesn't mean you should ignore their behaviors or reactions that cause a breakdown in communication. Take heart! Be honest with yourself about your contribution to the lack of respect, time spent, and communication in your marriage. Be honest with your spouse about your feelings, and take responsibility for your part. Plan actions you can take to strengthen and improve your relationship.

Unresolved conflict blocks intimacy. You have the ability to resolve conflicts one by one, removing the blocks. Ask, "What do you need from me? How can I help heal the pain you are experiencing?"

In preparation for a discussion that may cause conflict, write down the qualities in your spouse you are thankful for. As you make your list, you will gain a renewed sense of appreciation and respect for their strengths, and it will affect the tone you use discussing sensitive and important matters.

Most of all, take the time and space to analyze your heart and what you contribute to the relationship. What did you learn about your approach to disagreements from the last chapter? What areas of weakness do you need to face in yourself in the midst of conflict?

The following tips can assist in resolving conflict, if you will take the time to focus on them before discovering yourself in the middle of conflict. Remember, you cannot fix your spouse, but you can work on yourself, and you are the principal influence and trigger in your spouse's life.

Take a Break

When a partner is disappointed or expressing pain, an avalanche of emotions can flare up. Give the other person time to process their feelings if need be. Taking a moment to breathe can protect a marriage and make a permanent impact on your spouse's heart. When a person wants to remove themselves from an argument, it is typically because they want to spare the relationship from anger-driven words or actions.

I often hear a husband or wife say they want to protect their marriage by taking a break from an argument—a time-out to process emotions—but their spouse will not let them. Instead, they follow and continue to flood the other with arguments, which is destructive and unbeneficial. If you struggle with certain aspects of your communication style, consider finding your "space" to respond, rather than reflexively reacting.

People who do not want to take a break during the heightened emotions of a conversation typically want it resolved immediately and feel abandoned if the conversation ends, even temporarily, without resolution. For those reasons, it is helpful for the retreating spouse to give a time limit for how long the break will last. This gives both parties what they need. A break to process the conflict, and a time frame to know when the conversation will resume.

Take Responsibility

Following the break, the best way to come back into the conversation is to take responsibility. Taking responsibility using positive communication can help resolve conflict in a respectful way.

Use phrases such as:

"I can see how my response did not help you feel heard."

"I should not have reacted to your pain in anger."

"I know I did not listen as well as I should have and did not make you feel loved when you most needed to feel love."

When someone is sharing their heart, it is the listener's job to ask questions to ensure they understand what their spouse is sharing. Asking questions is sometimes difficult to remember to do, and requires practice until it is a part of your skill set.

Take Time for Introspection

Take time for self-examination concerning why you react the way you do. There is a reason. You may find it helpful to understand your reactions. Why do you become angry when you feel unheard? Perhaps when you were a child, it seemed no one listened to you and you felt invisible.

As an adult, when you feel someone is not listening to your point of view, you may be reacting to the current situation as well as a history of situations that made you feel unheard. The other person's failure to listen may be triggering a flood of emotions within you from your family of origin. You may have experienced the desire to be a priority and have your family's attention, but instead received neglect or abandonment.

By understanding the origin of the emotions you experience when you feel unheard, you will be empowered to act in a less reflexive way. What happens when you react? What are the consequences of your behavior?

Pay close attention. By changing your reaction to their deed, you produce a more desirable outcome. Is your action or response causing more distance in your relationship? Or is it helping draw you and your spouse back together in a bond of attachment and trust?

Habits for Resolving Conflict

Are the practices of handling conflict simple? Yes! Are those habits easy to create? No!

For example, a diet plan is customarily simple and straightforward. You may be focusing on counting calories, and you have a goal to keep the number of calories you eat below a certain quantity each day. That is a simple concept, but counting your calories and reaching your goal requires effort and discipline. It is easy to continue eating without regard for the number of calories, but you must be intentional if you want to reach your goal.

The same principals apply to handling conflict properly. It is easy to blame, yell, stomp away, or withdraw; however, those negative forms of communication create a toxic environment. If you want to reach your goal to peacefully resolve conflict, choose to build a beautiful, safe, and warm environment to openly communicate in.

Building the following habits in your life will help you prevent conflict from spinning into a long-term source of pain in your relationship. While these habits are "simple," making them a daily

part of your life—particularly during conflict—is testing.
1. Speak in a respectful manner.
2. State your feelings.
3. Resist the urge to blame.
4. Listen!
5. Acknowledge and empathize with your spouses' feelings.
6. Try to understand your spouse's pain.
7. Restate how you interpret your spouse's feelings.
8. Respond to your spouse's pain, not their anger.
9. Be kind.
10. Establish a goal for the communication.
11. Stay calm.
12. When you don't understand, ask questions.
13. Anticipate a peaceful resolution.
14. Treat your spouse as God's gift to you, even in conflict.
15. Provide and discuss solutions.
16. Try solutions together.
17. When communication is difficult, pray together.

We recently took a family vacation. While on that trip to the ocean, we were discussing the dangers of sharks near the shoreline and how aggressive they can be. Our son, Kyle, responded with, "I don't think sharks mean to be ferocious! They just want a hug and do not know how to ask!"

While we all found his comment humorous, I began to think about how there could be some truth to that statement, and how it could also be true in humans. Sometimes we react in anger when we are confused, need acceptance, need understanding, need mercy, and do not know how to ask for it.

If a discussion turns into conflict, both parties should spend time studying the interactions that led up to the conflict. By reflecting on the series of events leading up to a conflict, you can see the missed opportunities for communication that may have kept the conversation from spiraling into negativity.

Talk to your spouse about missed opportunities and how to address them in future conversations. Learn from your cycles of communication and use the insight you have gained to prevent the negative cycles in the future.

Write down a list of things that seem to work best for you and your spouse to manage conflict. Keep the list in a central location in your home, and refer to it when conflict is looming. Write down what you both know to do to make the relationship stronger. Refer to your list frequently. Remind each other what you have written down. From time to time, update your lists as your skills improve and your needs change, so your list remains relevant.

Love Wins Exercise

As you face conflict this week, try the following tips to resolve the controversy.

1. Practice taking a break from heated discussions to process your emotions.
2. Practice taking responsibility.
3. Take time for self-analysis.
4. Write out "I" statements that can help you communicate to your spouse what you are feeling.
5. Ask your spouse: "Have I done anything this week to unknowingly cause you pain?"
6. Which of the habits listed for resolving conflict do you need to implement into your life?

CHAPTER 9

Communicating Love

To make a difference in someone's life, you don't have to be rich, brilliant, beautiful, or perfect. You just have to care.
Mandy Hale

You create an atmosphere of intimacy and trust, or distance and betrayal, with every interaction. Are you communicating love and creating an atmosphere of acceptance in your relationship? You must be intentional with every decision you make to ensure you communicate love in your marriage.

Every single decision you make impacts the welfare of your marriage. Every conversation you have, how you handle relationships outside of the home, how you take care of yourself, how you choose to parent, how you approach your career, how serious you are about your relationship with God—all of these choices impact the health of your marriage.

If a man vow a vow unto the Lord or swear an oath to bind his soul with a bond; he shall not break his word, he shall do according to all that proceedeth out of his mouth.
Numbers 30:2

What were your vows? What did you promise your spouse while you dated, or on your wedding day? Have you lived up to your vows? Have you taken responsibility for the pain you caused if you failed to keep your vows?

You perhaps vowed to love, honor, cherish, and respect each other. You promised to be faithful in sickness and in health, and to put each other above all others.

The vows you make to God and your spouse are sacred oaths. Honoring those pledges with your life, your choices, and your communication is a commitment that will reap great reward. Honor your spouse, communicate love, and leave a heritage of integrity for your children. Learn to communicate love.

In this chapter, we will look at various ways to communicate love, including using active constructive responses, positive affirmations, respectful dialogue, and emotional and physical intimacy.

> *Death and life are in the power of the tongue:*
> *and they that love it shall eat the fruit thereof.*
> Proverbs 18:21 KJV

Active Constructive Responses

How do you respond when your spouse shares good news with you? Studies indicate your response to good news is telling about the health of your relationship. The way you respond when others share success with you will either directly build or weaken your relationships. Research in couples' relationships suggests that supporting your partner when good things happen is as important as supporting your partner when bad things happen.

In 2006, Shelly Gable, a psychological researcher, conducted a study on couples' responses to good news. She found young couples to discuss recent positive events in their lives. She focused on the partner's response to their significant other's good news. The study found that couples respond to each other's good news using one of the following types of responses:

Active Constructiveness: "That is exactly what you have worked for! I am so happy for you! What are your thoughts about transitioning to that position?"

Passive Constructiveness: "I hope that works out for you."

Active Destructiveness: "I'm not sure you are up for the challenges of a position like that."

Passive Destructiveness: "I really hope next week we are not understaffed again. This week was brutal!"

Active Constructive responses are the most supportive and kindest type. The other responses do not allow for moments of celebration, and rob the relationship of joy. An Active Constructive response allows both parties to enjoy the news, savor the success, share the joy, and bond. Active Constructive responding is a way of "turning toward" your spouse instead of turning away from them. Turning toward your spouse, both in celebration and difficult times, shows support and builds the relationship.

It is important to be authentic with your responses. A positive, but phony response is obvious and not constructive. If you find it difficult to give active and constructive responses, start asking questions that encourage the other person to talk about their news. This dialog gives you the opportunity to be more connected with the good news they are sharing.

Two months after the study, psychologists followed up with the couples and found that active constructive responding was a major factor determining if couples were still together or not. Couples who showed interest in their partner's success and happiness were more likely to be together.

In another study, Gable found that active constructive responding was also associated with more intimacy between partners and with a higher quality relationship. For some, active constructive responses come naturally. For others, this takes effort. It is worth the energy to carve out the skill of using active constructive responses to build a stronger relationship.

Let no corrupt communication proceed out of your mouth, but that which is good to the use of edifying, that it may minister grace unto the hearers.
Ephesians 4:29 KJV

Positive Affirmations

Do you tend to focus more on what does work in your marriage, or what does not work? It is human nature to focus on the negative, but this tendency results in teaching your spouse how *not* to communicate with or prioritize you.

When you acknowledge your spouse's efforts, you communicate love, safety, security, and priority. Focusing on the negative is not time well-invested. By focusing on what your spouse does right, you teach them how to love you, communicate with you, and to reach your heart.

Giving positive affirmations to your children is easy and comes naturally. If a toddler is learning to walk, do you criticize them if they can't walk without holding onto something? Do you reprimand them when they fall? No! You cheer on every effort! You are delighted with each attempt to walk! You support their efforts to reach this milestone in their lives. Toddlers thrive with support and encouragement. Their grinning face shows accomplished pride with every step they take. Surrounded with love and support, toddlers can feel they have been successful.

From time to time, you overlook and fail to acknowledge adults' efforts, even if they have improved. You are inclined to communicate angst when you are hurting or disappointed, versus affirming the positive aspects of relationships. Ignoring the positive can spin relationships into a cyclone of negativity.

Here's an example of how easy it is to focus on the negative and forget to acknowledge the positive.

A husband starts his wife's car on a cold winter morning so she can open the car door and commute to work in a warm vehicle. The same morning, he forgets to take out the trash. The wife does not acknowledge her husband's effort to make her comfortable and happy, but instead pounces on the fact that he did not take out the trash.

"I don't ask for much, why do you forget to take the trash out every single week? Why can't you just do that one thing for me?" She complains.

Imagine how her husband feels. What if she would have focused on the positive and ignored the negative instead?

"How thoughtful of you to warm my car! That was an awesome surprise!"

With a positive statement, one can focus on what is right in the relationship, which encourages positive behavior and brings no attention to the negative. When one feels their efforts make a difference, they are inclined to contribute more. When focus is placed on what is not working in the relationship, more negativity will spawn from that attention.

Communication is complicated and often derailed by making assumptions and overreacting with "always" and "never" statements. For example: You never listen to me. You always must get the last word. I always give in. You never come home in a good mood. First, the previous statements are not factual. They are attempts to make strong points in conversations. By using absolutes, you set yourself up for an argument. As soon as you say, "You always run late!" you have just opened the door for your spouse to spout off every time over the past week, month or year that they were on time. That is not a productive conversation but is guaranteed to happen with the wrong word choice. Make every effort to objectively understand what your spouse is communicating. Being patient in spousal reaction will allow time to decide on the response needed instead of simply giving a knee-jerk reaction. An angry response is foolish and destructive. Make efforts to understand what your spouse is feeling so every response to them is in a loving and caring manner.

A gentle answer turns away wrath, but a harsh word stirs up anger.
Proverbs 15:1

Winning at Love

Giving "gentle answers" seems simple enough; however, in the passion of opposing opinions, it is easier said than done. Giving a soft response when anger and resentment are heightened is very difficult. If you have tried it, you know the wisdom of Proverbs 15:1 shines through desperate moments of disconnection and disrespect. Messages of understanding allow respect and connection to grow. Couples who mutually respect each other avoid a cycle of sadness, withdrawal, anger, and loss of trust.

The best apology you can give your spouse is changed behavior! When you are motivated to please your spouse, you will take responsibility for the pain you caused, apologize and change your behavior accordingly.

Believe in your spouse and communicate your confidence in them aloud. Be vulnerable enough to admit when you are wrong. Do not continue to mentally rehearse the pain you experienced. Instead, share your feelings with your spouse. Be quick to extend grace. Be quick to forgive. Be the first to apologize.

Find solutions together. Are you becoming defensive? Do you storm out? Do you wall up and isolate yourself? All of these reactions are natural when you feel pain. The key is to determine what prompts your responses. Take the risk and talk about feelings instead of reacting to them. Discuss issues with your spouse. If you can problem solve together, you will feel more confident as a couple and more connected.

What do you love and appreciate about your spouse? Take the time and energy to share your thoughts on this with your spouse.

What are your favorite memories with them? Share those moments with them.

What do you love and appreciate about your marriage? Let your spouse know.

I call these constructive discussions "positive anchors" for your marriage. Some examples of positive anchors are: sharing a pleasant memory, recognizing some effort your spouse makes, complimenting an attribute, or giving encouragement.

Every large ship has massive anchors to add stability to the vessel. An anchor keeps a ship from drifting in the water's current, but is only effective if thrown out into the deep. The anchor must reach the ocean floor and sink into sand to stabilize the ship. Winds may come and toss the vessel, but the anchor keeps the ship where the captain wants it to be. Anchors offer security during storms and turbulent times.

Marriages need words and experiences that act as positive anchors for your relationship. You need words to stabilize your marriage when it feels uncertain, and words remind you why are here and why your commitment is important.

Positive words will stabilize communication when it feels hostile. Optimistic words will provide resolve when insecurity creeps into a relationship. Choose your words wisely. Clear-cut, confident words serve as the anchors to a marriage ship. Affirming, unquestionable words have a huge impact on the stability and security of the relationship during adversity or hardship.

Be assertive enough to use vulnerable words. Be brave enough to start conversations that matter. Intentionally use words that heal.

Marriage should be honored by all, and the marriage bed kept pure, for God will judge the adulterer, and all the sexually immoral.
Hebrews 13:4

Emotional and Physical Intimacy

Emotional intimacy is essential to creating healthier physical intimacy. You cannot be vulnerable physically if you are emotionally disconnected. Feeling safe enough to be emotionally vulnerable is the gateway to passion and physical intimacy.

Don't allow distractions to block emotional and physical intimacy. Children, busy schedules, illness, loss, and stress can impact the energy and time you place into your relationship. Intimacy is a private and personal area of your marriage and is worth every effort to maintain, insulate, and protect.

When you were dating, you took the time to know your sweetheart. You had long talks about every ambition, goal, and desire in your heart. You engaged in open discussions about positive and negative aspects of the relationship. When you married your spouse, you were confident that no one else on the planet could possibly make you as happy as they could! And you were the best candidate to make them content.

Why were you confident? Because you both knew exactly what the other needed to be happy—to experience emotional and physical intimacy. You knew what made your partner feel confident, secure, loved, needed, heard, and important, and you were excited to take on the challenge.

As the months and years passed, you forgot to get an update on your spouse's needs. You stopped taking time for long talks about what made each of you feel confident, secure, loved, needed, and listened to.

You do your best to do things you believe a husband or wife should do to build a marriage, but what if all your effort is in vain? If you don't know what each other's needs are, you are not fulfilling them. You might be surprised to find out your spouse has changed over time, and their needs have also changed. Communicating will make you better equipped to take on the challenge of pleasing them and making them feel treasured!

The gift of sexual intimacy in marriage is the magnet that draws you and your love to one another. God gave humans sexual desires and gave you a spouse to enjoy those pleasures with. Marriage is God's way of ensuring that you maintain emotional connection, physical relationship and shared passion. Sex is His way of giving your marriage private pleasure and an exclusive connection with one another. Selfless love, warmth and affection strengthens your marriage and your ability to connect physically and emotionally.

Love Wins Exercise

Plan a celebration for your spouse dedicated to an accomplishment they completed in the past year. It may be an achievement you made together, such as an anniversary, or reaching a financial goal. How can you verbally express an active constructive response about the success? What type of celebration would your spouse most enjoy?

Frequently ask your spouse: What can I do or say that will make you feel most loved?

Take the time today to sit down with your spouse and ask for an updated list of what they need from you to feel loved and to create an atmosphere to foster emotional and physical intimacy.

> *The end of a matter is better than its beginning,*
> *and patience is better than pride.*
> *Wisdom is a shelter as money is a shelter,*
> *but the advantage of knowledge is this:*
> *Wisdom preserves those who have it.*
> Ecclesiastics 7:8-8, 12-13

CHAPTER 10

Kindness

*Be kind and compassionate to one another,
forgiving each other, just as Christ forgave you.*
Ephesians 4:32

A study published in the *Journal of Marriage and Family* found that kindness and emotional stability are the most important predictors of satisfaction in a marriage. Kindness nurtures emotional intimacy and makes each partner feel loved and cared for. When you continue in unwavering kindness, instead of instability based on emotion, you will create a satisfying marital experience.

Couples who strive to build strong relationships have something in common. They enjoy each other's company and nurture their marriage with a spirit of kindness, forgiveness, and generosity. Kindness fosters an environment where one can learn new ways to bond with their spouse and savor happy moments.

John and Julie Gottman's research on couples is the most sought after and respected research for predicting the success of marriage. By observing marital interactions, they can predict with up to ninety four percent certainty if couples will remain happily together years later. Their study observes how each individual treats the other. Who is generous? Who is critical? Who is grateful? Who is full of contempt? Who is hostile? Who is kind?

"There's a habit of mind that [happily married couples] have," John Gottman explained in an interview. "They are scanning the social environment for things they can appreciate and say thank you for. They are building a culture of respect and appreciation very purposefully. Disasters are scanning the social environment for their partners' mistakes."

"It's not just scanning environment," chimed in Julie Gottman. "It's scanning the partner for what the partner is doing right or scanning him for what he's doing wrong and criticizing versus respecting him and expressing appreciation."

The Gottmans found that contempt is the number one factor that tears couples apart. If a couple is hyper-focused on criticizing their spouse, they miss fifty percent of the positive things their partner is doing. If contempt is present, a couple sees only negativity when there are positive things to focus on as well.

Contempt and criticism are not welcome allies for healing, forgiveness and love. Articulating and addressing pain or conflict is the bridge to healing the pain. The happiest couples are kind to one another, give grace, give the benefit of the doubt, and build one another up.

Gratefulness is one of the easiest routes for kindness. Gratefulness helps us focus on our spouse's positive traits. Focus on the qualities you fell in love with. Is your partner caring, diligent, loyal, faithful, devoted, industrious, kind, or affectionate? Reminding yourself of positive qualities and being grateful for those qualities allow for a reprieve to redirect energy.

Gratefulness does not change the fact that a situation may be less than ideal; however, it does help shift you away from downward emotional spirals and lifts you back to a positive, hopeful outlook.

*Be kind and compassionate to one another,
forgiving each other, just as Christ forgave you.*
Ephesians 4:32

Winning at Love

Can you think of a time recently when someone was kind to you? How did it impact your heart? How did it change your day? How did it impact your attitude? Kindness is powerful! But being kind when you have been hurt is difficult. Being kind opens the door of your heart to love and forgiveness.

Be kind and compassionate to one another,
forgiving each other, just as in Christ God forgave you.
Ephesians 4:32

One of my favorite Bible stories is about the poor widow who gave her last bit of oil away to God's servant. It was not just kindness, it was also a sacrificial act. The story is found in First Kings, chapter seventeen.

The passage provides insight about the prophet Elijah and gives the account of his interactions with a widow from Zarephath. The writing indicates the Lord was prohibiting rainfall in Israel. The nation's royal couple, Ahab and Jezebel, were leading their people into idolatry and the drought was God's judgment for their sin.

In verse eight, the Lord commanded Elijah to go to Zarephath where a widow would look after him and feed him. Elijah went to Zarephath. He found the widow woman gathering sticks. He said to her, "Bring me a little water in a vessel, that I may drink," and, "Bring me a morsel of bread in your hand."

The widow was in great need, desolate and out of food. When Elijah asked her to feed him, she was shocked. It would take the last bit of food she had in her little kitchen.

She responded, "As the LORD your God lives, I have nothing baked, only a handful of flour in a jar and a little oil in a jug. And now I am gathering a couple of sticks that I may go in and prepare it for myself and my son, that we may eat it and die."

She must have been heartbroken to know she was preparing the last meal for herself and her son. They had no other options for food. They were doomed to die.

Elijah told her to prepare food for him anyway. He instructed her to use the last of her ingredients for his meal, but added this: "For thus says the LORD, the God of Israel, 'The jar of flour shall not be spent, and the jug of oil shall not be empty, until the day that the LORD sends rain upon the earth'" (1 Kings 17:14).

What a promise. The widow obeyed and God was faithful to His promise.

"She and he and her household ate for many days. The jar of flour was not spent, neither did the jug of oil become empty, according to the word of the LORD that he spoke by Elijah" (1 Kings 17:15-16).

Her food supply was restored every day. She was able to eat and prepare food for herself, her son, and Elijah every day. In the middle of a nationwide famine, they never went without. God provided.

The widow willingly gave up her last portion of flour and last drops of oil to feed Elijah. She had amazing faith. She leaned on God's provision for her needs. Miraculously, because of her faith and obedience, God met her needs. Her kindness opened a floodgate of abundant blessings on her life. I wonder if she had not sacrificed how her story would have concluded. Would she and her son have died? What would have happened to Elijah?

The widow was not only kind to God's servant, she sacrificed for him. Because of her sacrifice, God blessed her with life. He spared her life and her son's life. I have confidence in God's love for you. He will give you a miracle when you sacrificially love others.

It may be a sacrifice to extend kindness to your spouse when your heart wants revenge. It may be a sacrifice to extend mercy to your spouse when you feel incapable of mercy. Trust God to meet you at your point of need. Trust Him to give you strength to sacrifice and extend mercy and kindness when your heart feels ill prepared to do so.

Consider Your Perspective

Perspective is everything. If you perceive your spouse has you under a microscope and is constantly judging you, you will allow insecurity and resentment to root in your heart. If you believe your spouse is doing the best they can, you will respect and encourage them. If you hold onto resentment because of your pain, you will continually look for more reasons to be disgruntled.

Believing the best in your spouse is one of the most powerful gifts you can give your marriage. Keeping your perspective positive indicates that you value your spouse and your marriage. Think about how you want to be treated. Doesn't it feel good when someone believes in you? A person can soar to their best when they receive verbal and emotional affirmation.

If you believe in your spouse, you offer grace and show them you understand they would never intentionally hurt you. It feels good to have someone believe the best in you. Believing in your partner provides a soft place to land and cultivates security in your marriage.

If you don't already believe in your partner, shifting your perspective may take some effort. Intentionally believing the best is worth the work, and it will breathe new life into your relationship, and will impact how you react to one another.

When Kindness is Difficult

Marriage was a decision you made, and God has entrusted you to love your spouse through thick and thin. Kindness is an expression of love. Kindness can be difficult to show your spouse when they are unlovable toward you.

Maintaining a disposition of kindness when your spouse has betrayed you is demanding. Staying kind when they have hurt you is trying. Embracing your spouse when they have disappointed you is taxing. When everything in you wants to run, kindness allows you the fortitude to stay and remain committed.

Many factors contribute to the failure of a marriage, but the disintegration of kindness quickly leads to the deterioration of a relationship. Couples can become overwhelmed by the stressors of life and allow responsibilities, work, family, friends, grief, or illness to overshadow their relationship. Stressors takeover the forefront, and kindness shifts lower on the list of priorities.

You may find yourself giving a cold shoulder to the person you vowed to honor and protect. Ignoring a spouse or barely giving an acknowledgment devalues them and is damaging. This action dishonors the vows made on your wedding day.

Oftentimes, unkind responses are a result of pain. It is critical to your marriage to talk about what you are experiencing internally, resolve emotional conflict, and heal from pain. Ignoring pain will eventually lead to that unresolved issue overwhelming the relationship, which leads to more emotional separation and isolation.

> *Be completely humble and gentle; Be patient, bearing with one another in love. Make every effort to keep the unity of the spirit through the bond of peace.*
> Ephesians 4:2-3

The most vital and yet difficult time to practice kindness is during conflict. Allowing contempt and aggression to spiral out of control and crush kindness causes additional damage to the relationship. During a conflict, you can deescalate the conversation by responding in kindness. The most natural human reaction is to mirror your spouse's words, tone, and presentation, but that is not always the wisest choice. Remember, if they are angry or upset, they are experiencing pain.

What if you started to care more about their pain than yours? Do you think caring about their pain will escalate the conflict? Absolutely not.

When you demonstrate kindness, care, and concern toward the cause of your spouse's pain, you turn toward them. When you exemplify kindness, you are not attempting to be correct, defending yourself, minimizing their pain, or explaining how wrong they are. When you display kindness, you pull your spouse toward you by caring about their heart. You have the ability to offer healing by making their pain a greater priority than yours and expressing empathy through kindness.

Above all, love each other deeply,
because love covers over a multitude of sins.
1 Peter 4:8 NIV

Love Wins Exercise

Plan a date night where you and your spouse both share a list of seven things you admire about each other. Repeat this activity at least once every six to eight weeks. Looking forward to your spouse's list causes anticipation and delight!

CHAPTER 11

Perseverance

*Attitude is the librarian of our past,
the speaker of our present and the prophet of our future.*
John Maxwell

Is your life the way you envisioned it would be when you were twenty years old? In some ways, it may be better than you could have ever envisioned.

Maybe, you could not have imagined loving as deeply as you love today. You probably couldn't imagine the deep well of joy your children bring into your life. Maybe you feel a strong sense of satisfaction from accomplishing goals, completing degrees, or achieving success in your career.

You probably had no idea how accomplished you would feel when you closed on your first house and drove away with the keys to your new safe haven. What a wonderful feeling! You couldn't know how great it would feel because you lacked the life experience to understand the impact these moments would have on your life.

You had no idea the gamut of emotions you would experience when you held your baby for the first time. Do you remember how you studied your child's face, looking for hints of your own genetics, and watching in amazement at each yawn, or as tiny fingers wrapped around yours? Think about the moments you will never forget, the moments that changed you forever.

As a twenty-year-old, you could not possibly have comprehended the accomplishment of twenty-five years of marriage to someone who loves you and has your best interest at heart. You had no idea the value of a friendship that has weathered thirty years of tears, laughter, celebrations, births, and deaths. You had no idea the impact that every choice you made through the years would have on your life.

You also had no idea how much tenacity and determination you would need to forge forward to persevere in life and marriage. You had no idea of the obstacles, and nothing could prepare you for them. You did not envision losing jobs, opportunities, relationships, or self-esteem. You did not imagine the people who would fail you, disappoint you, lie about you, or betray you.

You can either allow your experiences to destroy you, or you can decide to use your brokenness to strengthen your resolve to live more passionately. You can choose to live with more purpose, and with more determination to make a difference in the lives of the people you love, and those who love you.

Winning at Love

When you have been married thirty or forty years, you have the marriage thing figured out, don't you? Amazingly, no. You have many years of experience in understanding each other, selflessly loving one another, forgiving, and compromising, but nothing prepares you for the next hurdle.

It may be a health situation, the death of a child or grandchild, financial distress, or watching an adult child struggle. I see many couples whose adult child is experiencing legal problems, in prison, entrenched in addiction, or going through a job loss. Sometimes an adult child moves back in with their parents for an extended period. Often, grandparents gain custody of their grandchildren when the parents are not capable of giving their children adequate care.

Your life may not be how you envisioned it would be, and it may feel overwhelming to take on the responsibility of an adult child as well as any children they may have. Oftentimes, one spouse is determined to step in and help their child, and the other is stanch in the belief that their child needs tough love and they must love from a distance.

Marital conflict may begin with differing opinions and the stress that these situations bring into a couple's life. If a child or grandchild moves into the home, the additional stress can be unnerving.

One beautiful couple I treated had been married for forty-five years. Sue and Brian both retired from very prestigious careers. They planned to continue living in their affluent, settled neighborhood in Nashville. Then, their thirty-four-year-old daughter, Mandi, went through a divorce. The divorce was bitter. Mandi's ex-husband did not maintain a relationship with their two children. Mandi had the full responsibility to care for two preteen boys who were both were severely autistic. She homeschooled the boys because it was difficult for them to function in the public-school setting.

Sue and Brian realized Mandi could not manage her household and the responsibilities of her boys. They decided to sell their gorgeous home and buy a larger home to accommodate Mandi and the boys. It was a huge sacrifice for them. It was a lot of change at one time to take on so much responsibility during a time they had envisioned a slower pace of life.

My heart broke for them as I heard them share their shattered dreams of retirement, of giving up a home they loved in a neighborhood they enjoyed and were well-connected in. It was sad for them to trade their quiet life for one where they constantly worked to cook, clean, and provide for five people.

Sue and Brian felt guilty for having ill feelings toward the sacrifice and the life changes would demand of them. They were sad because they didn't feel their efforts were appreciated. They both reacted to the stressors differently, which caused even more stress their relationship.

It had been a long time since their marriage relationship was this stressed. In forty-five years, they had weathered job losses, deaths in the family, illnesses, parenting differences, challenging friendships, and financial difficulties. They found solace for their relationship by praying together. They had forty-five years of standing tall in the face of storms, but now they were tired. They were weak. They felt unappreciated. And they didn't know what to do.

Their sacrifice was admirable! I was impressed at the lengths they had gone to ensure security for their daughter and grandchildren. However, it seemed their willingness to help was more expected than appreciated.

We worked on building boundaries. They needed healthier boundaries with their daughter and grandchildren. They also needed to carve out their own lives in the middle of the chaos. Their daughter and her boys were scripting their daily schedules, and Sue and Brian were losing their privacy and the ability to maintain their own schedule and social life.

Giving them permission to feel overwhelmed and unappreciated allowed them to have a safe place to feel weariness without guilt. They found a fresh perspective and felt like a team again.

They set goals, planned couple time, determined to establish house rules, and allowed themselves not to feel constantly at the service of their family members. They learned to love their family enough to expect them to do for themselves and give each one of them daily responsibilities.

Taking these steps gave Sue and Brian control of their home again and allowed them to continue to give without resentment or feeling they were expected to give. Now they could give with joy. Their marriage relationship was more unified and they began enjoying their retirement. It still was not the retirement they had dreamed of, but they were devoted to the welfare of their family and they were happy to be able to assist. They committed to and found a path for enjoying their lives. Finding their commitment to boundaries with their family gave them freedom to enjoy their home again. We can all learn from their courage and perseverance.

A river cuts through a rock
not because of its power, but its persistence!
Zig Ziglar

It's All About Attitude

Perhaps you have looked at the marriages around you and determined your marriage is not as loving, exciting, or romantic as others. Reality is not always the same as what we perceive it to be. Comparison is a trap that robs you of the ability to appreciate your journey, relationships, and blessings.

Focusing on other relationships does not effectively use your energy to build a great relationship in your own life. Do not become distracted. If your goal is to have a stronger marriage, put your energy toward your goal, and commit to persevere.

An attitude of perseverance is also one of preparation. Prepare to fight battles and to face unexpected storms and difficult times. Commit to moving forward with your partner. Bind together in prayer, and allow God to strengthen your resolve.

The enemy of your soul uses isolation and division to separate you from your spouse and open your marriage to extreme vulnerability. When you are at your weakest, he pounces with temptation, conflict, disgust, insecurity, jealousy, betrayal, and a host of other relationship toxins.

If you find yourself confused by circumstances, it is possible you are facing a spiritual attack. Before a person ever says, "I do," their ideas about marriage are under attack. "Entertainment" mocks traditional family values and glamorizes sin. American culture floods society with deceitful images promoting sexual promiscuity, adultery, premarital sex, and prostitution. These are all reasons it is important to emphasize the spiritual aspects of marriage, and the importance of keeping God first in your life.

Even the way Hollywood romanticizes relationships is destructive to the foundation of marriage, as marriage is not always sexy or glamorous. Our society makes marriage seem disposable. Often a spouse will ask me, "Should marriage be this hard?" There is a false notion that if the relationship were "right," you would not need to struggle to make it work. That simply could not be further from the truth!

Movies portray couples basking in love and admiration for one another in paradise, with their children joyfully tucked in bed. Fast forward to the next scene where perfection ends and divorce is the next stop. *Divorce is not the answer to an imperfect marriage; perseverance is the key to reclaiming your joy.*

Perseverance calls us to continue fighting for our God-given relationship. Often, simply acknowledging the fact that God called you to your marriage can provide the strength you need to persevere through hardship. Your commitment to God will set the pace when your emotions want to give up. With an attitude of perseverance, you can equip yourself with the tools and resources to withstand difficult times. Surround yourself with godly influences that will speak into your life, encouraging and building up your relationship with God and your spouse.

Life can be difficult but you were built for this. Every event in your life has prepared you for this battle. What you are going through right now is your testimony in the making.

Whatever you do, do it with all your heart,
as working for the Lord, not for human masters.
Colossians 3:23

The grace of the Lord Jesus Christ be with your spirit.
Philippians 4:23

The Big Picture

Perseverance ultimately involves increasing safety, empathy, security, and responsiveness. There is no magic potion to persevere through difficult times in relationships. Intimacy must be pursued through the storms of life. Unfortunately, intimacy is not automatically installed or downloaded into our hearts when we sign a marriage contract. We must work for closeness and constantly make efforts to pursue emotional and physical intimacy.

Stepping into a new terrain and shifting to a more vulnerable and emotional level is imperative for change to occur. When one partner aggressively emphasizes resentment, or withdraws into emotional paralysis, the other partner may react in a similar way. During a negative cycle, partners may feel misunderstood, alienated, and unsupported.

Couples must face pain together, and intentionally pursue respect and connection to grow together and heal from hurt. Communicating vulnerably and honestly requires commitment and effort. Making the effort to communicate will help restructure unhealthy patterns of interaction. When one partner communicates non-defensively after feeling misunderstood, it tends to result in mutual respect, and emotional togetherness. After learning a new cycle of communication, couples will be eager to maintain the new, healthier patterns.

To condition your relationship to persevere, communication must increase so intimacy can deepen. Vulnerability and understanding must abound, and knee-jerk reactions must diminish. Growth and healing occur in intimacy as two people lay down their defenses and connect in safe and constructive ways. At times, both spouses may be committed to each other and the marriage, but are still stuck in destructive cycles that overwhelm their senses. If that is the case, therapy is a great way to develop new skills and tools to persevere. As a couple equips themselves to persevere in marriage, they will be more likely to turn toward one another throughout all of life.

Many individuals struggle to manage intense reactive emotions during conflict. Reactions determine the connection couples feel toward each other. If you and your partner find yourselves in a tailspin of disconnection, lean into a new mentality intentionality marked and driven with respect and understanding.

Love Wins Exercise

Here is a great exercise you and your spouse can do together. I call it "Four Things." Each time you practice this exercise, you will need to select a topic, theme, or question.

Some examples of a topic, theme, or question include: What do you love about me? Where do you want to travel? What are your favorite vacation memories? Perfect date ideas? What about me inspires you? What have I done this week that reminds you I love you?

Throughout the week, whenever you or your spouse comes up with a theme, you both must come up with "Four Things" to match the topic.

For example, if your spouse calls out, "Four Things! Thankfulness." You would list four things you are thankful for. Then your spouse would do the same.

The next time, you may say, "Four Things! Memories!" At that time, your spouse would list four favorite memories, and then you would do the same.

Four Things is easy, fun, and can be done anywhere. Use your imagination and be creative!

CHAPTER 12

Forgiveness

*Happy marriages begin when we marry the ones we love,
and they blossom when we love the ones we marry.*
Tom Mullen

A betrayal, mistreatment, lie, or any other disloyalty is a tall order to forgive. When your heart is broken and your trust in the relationship is shattered, you likely have a laborious climb ahead of you to reach the place where you are ready to forgive. In fact, you may never be ready to forgive. Forgiveness is an intentional choice you need to make regardless of your feelings.

Do not mistake forgiveness for pretending you are not too disappointed or upset. Forgiveness is not an excuse to ignore problems in your marriage, nor is it meant to negate taking responsibility for unhealthy patterns within the marriage. Forgiveness puts a boundary on the conflict within your heart. Forgiveness doesn't change what hurt you in the past, but it does give hope for your future.

Winning at Love

One of the most incredible things about being a counselor is watching forgiveness transform brokenness into hope. It is miraculous to watch a person who is tormented by some injustice release their pain, hate, and wrath, as God fills their heart with mercy, grace, and compassion.

One client I was honored to work with was a sweet mom I'll call "Samantha." She was grieving the loss of her eighteen-month-old son "Ethan." She divorced her husband six months prior to her son's death, due to his alcoholism and the lifestyle choices he made in his addictive state of mind.

Although they were divorced, her ex-husband still had visitation rights to their son every other weekend. One weekend, the visit turned into tragedy. Samantha's ex-husband put their son to sleep in his bed. The man drank a lot that night and passed out in the bed. At some point during the night, he rolled over on his son and accidentally suffocated him. Everyone's lives changed that night.

Samantha was in a rage. Her son was her life, and his life was stolen. She sat across from me gripping Ethan's stuffed bear. She would bury her head into the bear and scream and sob. Her grief was raw and emotional. For months, we worked through her pain. When I would talk to her about forgiveness, she resisted. How could she forgive such an egregious act? How could she forgive the person who took her son's life?

She said repeatedly that she could not forgive. It was too much to ask of her to lose her son and then forgive the one responsible as well. But she realized she was stuck. She couldn't heal around unforgiveness. She had to walk through her pain so she could lay down the burden of injustice she was carrying. There was no other path to healing. She must forgive.

Forgiveness was a very gut-wrenching, painful process of surrender. Surrendering ideas of justice, and remembering God is in control was vital to her process. God had not missed one moment of her anguish, heartbreak, or disappointment. He is just, and can be trusted with any betrayal, bitterness, or grievance.

Samantha courageously forgave her ex-husband. It was challenging journey. She could look ahead once she forgave. She was capable of dreaming again. She still had many pieces of life to put back together, and with God's help she would. Ethan would always be in her heart and she had the hope of Heaven which strengthened her on her weakest days.

Whatever you hold onto from the past ties you to the pain or failure. Choose freedom. Choose to be whole.

The miracle of forgiveness has an incredible impact on your heart. It cultivates your heart in ways you may not expect. Forgiveness gives you the capacity to hope again. Forgiveness allows you to see how the situations that hurt you the most, shapes your heart. You learn more about yourself, life, and love through painful circumstances. They serve a purpose and help you grow in your understanding of God's grace.

Dead Weight

One of the most gruesome practices of the Roman Empire was how they punished guilty criminals. Spitting, beating, and crucifixion were among the top choices. One punishment most appalling to me was the punishment reserved for the criminals of the most horrific crimes.

The Romans would strap a dead corpse onto the back of heinous criminals. For the rest of their lives, they carried around a decomposing corpse. The stench was overwhelming.

Toxic poisons from the corpse would drain into the criminal's skin pores. The person became sicker daily and died a slow, gruesome, painful death. It was a horrific way to die. The practice is where the term "dead weight" comes from.

For us, carrying dead weight means to carry something that has no purpose and causes harm. What is your dead weight? What are you carrying that will destroy you? What has caused you so much harm, yet you still refuse to release it? What pain is so important you are willing to risk your own well-being to rehearse the details and constantly relive the pain?

Sometimes we hold onto our inability to forgive because it feels as if we are punishing the other person by not forgiving them. We aren't punishing our spouse at all. Our partner may recognize a difference in the relationship, may notice a withdrawal or somber disposition, but may not realize unforgiveness is responsible for the shift in the relationship. If you are the partner carrying resentment, you are carrying dead weight.

Did the offense you are carrying happen last week, last month, or ten years ago? Do you feel better carrying it? Does it make you feel healthier, or stronger?

We know from the example of the corpse, carrying dead weight doesn't make you stronger; in fact, it weakens and destroys you!

Are you carrying bitterness, resentment, or unforgiveness? Each of these are a dead weight, a corpse that will have a tragic effect on you. Dead weight destroys your hopes, dreams, relationships, and ambitions. You will not be an overcomer by carrying around a corpse of unforgiveness. You cannot find joy and peace while grasping the corpse of bitterness and resentment.

Your need for justice will overwhelm you with thoughts of how unfair life is. Toxic attitudes and behaviors will pour out of your heart and destroy you.

Do you want peace? Make time to create a space in your heart for letting go. People around you can sense your heart is filled with disappointment and pain. They smell defeat, which has a very identifiable odor.

Intentionally determine to forgive, and take back your life, your family, and your marriage. What corpse is killing your marriage? What corpse is killing you? Once you identify the corpse, unstrap it from your heart, set it down, and offer forgiveness for the injustice. Set yourself free to live.

> *Blessed is the one who perseveres under trial because,*
> *having stood the test, that person will receive the crown*
> *of life that the Lord has promised to those who love Him.*
> James 1:12

Unhealed Wounds

James Garfield was elected President of the United States in 1880, but only served in office for six months. Someone shot him in the back very early in his administration, and he spent the next six months under the care of a host of physicians.

Doctors poked and prodded him, feverishly trying to locate and retrieve the bullet, but no one could find it. Garfield died six months later, but the gun wound is not what killed him. The doctor's continual probing did not save his life, it killed him. He died from infection.

Relationships are vulnerable to pain. Pain becomes even more deeply rooted in a marriage when partners choose not to forgive. Blame, accusation, belittlement, debate, and continuing to rehash and discuss past incidents that caused anguish buries the pain even further.

When you do not forgive, you cannot heal. Just like the story of President James Garfield, the continual poking and prodding of an unforgiven wound will cause an infection to set into your marriage. If your relationship becomes infected, toxic, sick, or septic, eventually your hope will be destroyed.

When You Can't Heal

Even with significant marriage goals, hearts full of love, and full intention to stay committed, you may still face insurmountable pain in your marriage, and situations too big to handle. Your hearts may be ragged from betrayal, loss, infidelity, addiction, disappointment, disease, physical impairment, or brokenness. The damage may seem irreparable. Some wounds require blind faith and trust in God to do what you cannot do for yourself and your marriage.

What mountain in your marriage is unsurmountable? What triggers fear, anger, lack of forgiveness, or resentment in your heart? God redeems pain. He takes great joy in restoring hope when you trust Him with your most desperate situation. Don't give up. Surrender your situation to God in prayer. By faith, forgive. By faith, love unconditionally. By faith, respect. By faith, continue to give.

> *Be joyful in hope, patient in affliction, and faithful in prayer.*
> Romans 12:12

Surrender your will, your knowledge, and your marriage to God. He has your life in His hands. Prayer will shape your destiny. Take the huge leap into God's will for your marriage, your future, and pray for your spouse, for your marriage, and for the future of your family.

Leave your children a beautiful legacy of prayer and steadfast commitment to God and marriage. There is power in surrender that only comes through prayer. Become an extension of God's grace and mercy, and you will see the impact it has on your spouse. When you extend grace to your partner, you will reap much more than you sow into the relationship.

By providing space to allow yourself to forgive and heal, you are refusing to allow pain to continue destroying your heart and marriage. By choosing to quickly forgive, you block pain from collapsing the strength that supports your marriage. Forgiveness allows your heart to sort through the problems, the pain, and disappointment. Forgiveness allows you to dig deep and find the courage to heal your brokenness with God's strength.

Jesus has set us free and forgiven us. Holding onto the truth of His forgiveness for you will give you the strength and valor to forgive your spouse. Surrendering your pain to God will empower you to create an atmosphere poised for restoration.

There are many things to remember throughout this journey. Never be too busy to be kind. Never be too broken to offer forgiveness. Never be too disappointment to experience joy. Never be too hopeless to have faith. Never be too busy to care about your spouse.

Never be so self-absorbed you forget to share. Never allow bitterness to overtake gentleness. Never be so broken you lose compassion. Never allow despair to overshadow hope. Never allow hate to fill a heart that is meant to be consumed with joy and love.

Love Wins Exercise

At least once a week, find time to nurture your marriage by praying together. Pray over your spouse aloud. Yes, praying aloud may feel vulnerable or foreign to you if you have never done it before. If you have prayed aloud together before, you understand the importance of creating a safe space for prayer in your marriage.

You will strengthen your spouse by your prayers. Your marriage will experience growth and emotional intimacy through heartfelt prayer. Making praying together a priority will restore hope, intimacy, love, and peace to your relationship.

Being strengthened with all power according to his glorious might so that you may have great endurance and patience. And giving joyful thanks to the Father who has qualified you to share in the inheritance of His holy people in the kingdom of light.
Collossians 1:11-12

CHAPTER 13

Pursue & Recover It All!

Not everything that is faced can be changed.
But nothing can be changed until it is faced.
James Baldwin

Your marriage is a gift from God. God designed marriage to enrich your life and bring glory to Him. The enemy of your soul will oppose anything that brings glory to God; that's the nature of the spiritual battle our fallen world is in.

The enemy loves to create division, divorce, and discord. He is aggressive, but we are armed with tools to win the battle. *Love Wins!*

Make a commitment to better communication, and to pray with and for one another. Prayer goes a long way in shutting down the enemy and his plan for destruction. If you are humble enough to pull down your defenses and work with your spouse, your marriage will be restored and you will protect your family.

Winning at Love

One couple I counsel came to me with so much brokenness. "Sandra" was grieving the loss of her mother. She had been her mom's primary caretaker since her dad died ten years prior. She was very close to her mom. Her mom died three months before Sandra started coming to counseling.

Her grief was overwhelming, and all her relationships were suffering. Her husband "Jim" was not patient regarding her grief. He thought his wife was remarkably emotional about her loss. His lack of concern and empathy only drove Sandra further from Jim.

Jim was sad about the loss of his mother-in-law, but he was also excited about the future and the fact that he and Sandra could make plans and travel without considering the care of her mom. Sandra found Jim's conversations about making plans absurd. How could she possibly find joy or make plans for fun in her time of loss. The gap in their communication widened and amplified the pain she was already experiencing.

Focusing on what Jim and Sandra needed as a couple was paramount. They needed joint goals. Jim needed to stop telling Sandra how to grieve and allow her to process her anguish. He needed to be supportive through her brokenness. Sandra had to learn that dreaming again was healthy. Dreaming together was strengthening for their marriage. As Jim began listening and sincerely caring about how Sandra was experiencing her grief, they both began to feel their relationship strengthen.

Do not underestimate the power of positive, encouraging words toward your spouse. When you believe in your spouse, express it. When you are thankful for them, let them know. When they love you well, say so. Your vulnerability will revive security and connection. *Listening is the loudest voice you can have in your marriage. Use it and use it often.*

> *Gracious words are a honeycomb,*
> *sweet to the soul and healing to the bones.*
> *There is a way that appears to be right,*
> *but in the end it leads to death.*
> Proverbs 16:24-25

It takes courage to heal. Only a brave heart is willing to face their darkest secrets and most dreaded conversations. It takes guts to talk about the moments you feel most rejected, unloved, and betrayed, especially without a guarantee that their vulnerability will redeem the brokenness in their relationship.

David's Distress

1 Samuel 30:1-10. David and his men reached Ziklag on the third day. Now the Amalekites had raided the Negev and Ziklag. They had attacked Ziklag and burned it, and had taken captive the women and everyone else in it, both young and old. They killed none of them, but carried them off as they went on their way.

When David and his men reached Ziklag, they found it destroyed by fire and their wives and sons and daughters taken captive. So, David and his men wept aloud until they had no strength left to weep. David's two wives had been captured—Ahinoam of Jezreel and Abigail, the widow of Nabal of Carmel. David was greatly distressed because the men were talking of stoning him; each one was bitter in spirit because of his sons and daughters. But David found strength in the LORD his God.

Then David said to Abiathar the priest, the son of Ahimelek, "Bring me the ephod." Abiathar brought it to him, and David inquired of the LORD, "Shall I pursue this raiding party? Will I overtake them?"

"Pursue them," he answered. "You will certainly overtake them and succeed in the rescue."

David and the six hundred men with him came to the Besor Valley, where some stayed behind. Two hundred of them were too exhausted to cross the valley, but David and the other four hundred continued the pursuit.

"David was greatly distressed."

David left his city unguarded, and returned to find it burned to the ground. The enemy came in and ravaged his city. His family was gone, the wives, sons, and daughters of his men were all captives. Little Ziklag, where they had made a home, was blackened ruins.

Wounded in heart, his people surrounded him, ready to stone him. They no longer trusted him because they too had lost everything they worked for. David's life was at the lowest point imaginable.

David had been acting without consulting God. He had a servant's heart, and usually waited on the Lord for direction. Even as a young boy, he would sing about listening to God's voice, and obeying God's will, but David made decisions without God directing him, and had chosen the wrong road.

Exhausted by Saul's persecution, in a weak moment he said, "I shall surely fall one day by the hands of Saul." He was in a precarious place emotionally, succumbed to the idea of failure, and was despondent. He forgot from where his strength came.

His spiritual life was weak and it directly affected his mood and capacity to make good decisions. When you are disconnected from God's direction and voice, sin can overtake you. When David stood in the ashes of Ziklag, he began to understand what a mistake it was to lean on his understanding. As he looked at the ruins of the disaster, he went to God to ask for help. *He strengthened himself in the Lord his God.*

Perhaps you, like David, are experiencing distress. You have chosen your path and now you are caught in a web of confusion. It looks as though you are going to lose everything. Your life is in ruins. Your heart is broken and you are dismayed when you look ahead. You are looking at your situation with your natural eyes. Consider God's voice. What does He say about the destruction and ruins surrounding you?

When David considered what action he should take, he asked God for direction.

And David enquired at the Lord, saying, Shall I pursue after this troop? shall I overtake them? And he answered him, Pursue: for thou shalt surely overtake them, and without fail recover all.
1 Samuel 30:8 KJV

David asked God, "What shall I do? Shall I pursue and overtake them?"

God answered him immediately, "Pursue! Overtake! Without fail you will recover all."

God moved David into a new season in his life where strength undergirded his weakness and allowed him success in places he failed.

There is a purpose for every season in your life. Just because you are in a season of failure, conflict, distress, or separation, does not mean this is how your story ends. Trust God with your failures. Allow Him to breathe life back into the brokenness of your choices. Surrendering to God is the key.

Find a place deep in your heart where you are willing to give up your plans for God's perfect plan. That doesn't mean you are perfect, or that your spouse is perfect, or that your life will be perfect. It does mean God has a perfect plan for all the imperfection you bring to Him.

What can you surrender? What failure, disappointment, injustice, or betrayal are you clinging to? What negative situation are you allowing to define your marriage? When you surrender that portion of your marriage, God can do a healing work in your life. If you refuse to surrender, you are choosing a path of brokenness.

Pursue! Overtake! Without fail you will recover it all!

Moving toward restoration in your marriage is not a natural process. You will fight every mental battle imaginable when you commit to healing your marriage. Pain paralyzes you, attempting to disarm your hope that healing is possible.

When you are in pain, your internal dialogue often shifts to "I deserve to be happy. I deserve more love than this marriage gives." These thoughts disrupt attempts to reconcile or offer forgiveness for betrayal or disappointment. Your commitment to the relationship must be more resolute than the toxic thoughts attempting to dissuade you. Even in your deepest pain, joy can triumph and overturn the death sentence on your relationship.

Infuse your schedule with down time together, activities you both enjoy that allow you to relax, laugh, and reconnect. Plan to watch funny movies that bring laughter into your relationship. Make time to play board games, or go on a trip together. Start dating each other again. Make sure you are loving each other well, forgiving each other, and accepting each other. Your human nature may naturally seek out the negative in your spouse. Be intentional about seeking the positive in your marriage.

It may be silly, but since the beginning of our marriage, my husband and I have a daily competition for who is "the sweetest." We try to outdo one another in acts of service and kindness to each other. Throughout the day, we teasingly remark that a comment or gesture should guarantee us the "sweetest award." It is a lighthearted, fun way to see the good in each other, and in our relationship.

Find your path for seeking the best in each other. Find a way to ensure that every day you are pursuing honor in your relationship. Find a way to ensure your focus is on the positive traits of your spouse and your marriage.

Don't forget to have fun. In the busy and stressful pace of careers, family, parenting, community leadership roles and other commitments, it is easy to lose sight of the joy of marriage. It's time to slow down.

Reach deep and find that reservoir of courage and perseverance to invest in your marriage. Understand that you are not just fighting for your marriage but you are fighting for future generations. You are conquering mountains and setting the precedent for the next generation. *Pursue! Overtake! Without fail you will recover it all!*

I pray God undergirds you with strength and resilience that you have never experienced before. I pray that the words of this book become a force in your spirit that is undeterred!

Love Wins Exercise

Create a daily connecting point with your spouse. A connect point doesn't have to be a twenty-minute discussion; it may only be five minutes of sharing your heart. In those moments, seek to connect with your spouse emotionally, spiritually, and physically.

Check their heart, reassure them of your devotion, care, and concern for their wellbeing. Your connect point may include a lingering hug, a passionate kiss, or appreciating each other's eyes, and speaking kind words. Keep your marriage full of an abundance of hugs, and passionately kiss daily.

CHAPTER 14

A Beacon of Hope

Coming together is a beginning,
keeping together is progress,
working together is success.
Henry Ford

A strong marriage is a beacon of hope for the world. Your marriage is an opportunity to shine God's love. It is one of the most wonderful ways you and your spouse can serve humankind. We live in tumultuous times where the world is cloaked in dark defeat and shattered dreams. Your marriage can shine the bright light of God's love into the darkness.

Strong marriages benefit children by providing an unwavering foundation for their lives. We begin building our beliefs about marriage very early in life. By learning from our parents, grandparents, and other significant couples in our lives, we begin understanding roles for men and women, and learning how they fall in love, marry, and start a family. Your children, and everyone around you, desperately need to see role models who prove creating a faithful, sincere, and selfless marriage is possible.

A strong Christian marriage is a witness for Christ. It is a joy to celebrate the treasure of a God-given marriage. Marriage was God's plan from the beginning to bring completion, companionship, and to enrich life. Through marriage, we can learn more about God's love for us than in any other relationship.

Marriage is strong when determination overshadows fear.

For I am the Lord your God who takes hold of your right hand
and says to you, "Do not fear, I will help you."
Isaiah 41:13

Winning at Love

One spring day, a lovely couple came to me for their initial session. "Alexis" and "Mike" were both successful professionals. They had been married for eight years, but had grown distant the past two years. Unresolved conflict caused distance in their relationship.

Mike had a friend at work who was going through difficult times in her relationship. Mike and the woman at work started sharing their struggles and disappointments. They found comfort in each other's company and appreciated the understanding and acceptance they found in one another. Before long, the friendship became a relationship and they began a romantic affair.

Alexis felt isolated and separated from Mike, but was unsure why and didn't know what to do about it. She noticed a text on his phone that alerted her he was not being faithful to their marriage. She was devastated.

Their relationship was already in disorder. She immediately asked Mike for a divorce. Mike was disappointed in himself and the choices he was making, but still wanted to save his marriage and convinced Alexis to go to counseling.

So, there they were in front of me. They were married, yet felt worlds apart.

Their pain was almost tangible. They had no hope. They poured out their grief and despair. Alexis shared her feelings of betrayal, distrust, disappointment, and anguish. Mike shared his feelings of shame, guilt, rejection, and isolation.

Initially, our focus was on Alexis and Mike listening to each other share their pain, each showing validation, and allowing the healing to begin. Mike needed to understand what made him vulnerable to betraying his marriage vow. He feared not being successful in his career and in his marriage. He allowed his fears to predict his behavior, which destroyed something he treasured. Alexis needed to focus on forgiveness and evaluating her role in the state of the relationship before dealing with Mike's affair.

Counseling was a journey for them. They shared their thoughts on feeling shame, resentment, unloved, rejected, and disrespected. We dove into the negative emotions in an effort to heal their hearts: rejection, sadness, anger, fear, insecurity, abandonment, and more. Healing deep wells of pain begins when your spouse listens without defending their actions. This courageous couple stood up to the challenge and diligently worked to find restoration. Gradually, they began to accept hope. They started believing that they had the capacity to heal.

They also decided to attend church again. They enjoyed their commitment to church early in their marriage, but responsibilities distracted them and they wavered in their faith commitments. They shared that making their spiritual walk a priority again helped restore hope in their hearts for their marriage to heal. They found safety in their marriage again.

Mike and Alexis now have a beautiful, loving, and secure marriage. I am so thankful to have been a small part of their emotional healing, as well as in many other similar journeys.

Marriage is not easy. We need God's help.

Human nature is primed with selfishness and sinful desires that can easily give way to infidelity and betrayal. If you want to protect your marriage, each partner must focus on building their individual relationship with God. Marriage requires hard work and devotion, not only to each other, but to God.

Surrendering your desires through prayer allows God to shape your heart and order your steps. Healing a broken heart begins with surrender. God is able to remove layers of selfishness, unforgiveness, contempt, and blame, and replace all of that with hope. Just as Christ is the hope of our salvation and life, He is also the hope of our marriages.

Distorted expectation occurs when one partner expects their spouse to give them what comes from God: identity, security, or self-esteem. If you look to your spouse, family, or children to fulfill needs that only God can fill, it puts enormous pressure on a family and sets a marriage up for failure. Having unrealistic expectations will keep you disappointed. Find yourself, your confidence, your meaning, and purpose for life within your relationship with God. When God is first, it allows you to be healthy and enjoy a connected marriage relationship.

Pray together, fast together, and study God's Word together. It is difficult to be angry at a person you are praying for and with. Allow God to temper your words, and give you a gentle spirit. Speak with kindness and use tone filled with grace and mercy. Pick up your cross and follow Jesus as you walk with your spouse through life.

In uncertain times, the best you can do is face today bravely, trust God and move step-by-step in the direction God leads you. You don't have to understand to trust God. You don't have to have all the answers to trust God. You don't even have to feel a sense of certainty to trust Him. That's why we call it faith. The more you find you cannot do, the more room there is for God to do. *Forge forward, together in Christ! Have confidence in the Lord!*

If God is for us, who can be against us?
Romans 8:31

The more intimately you love, the more vulnerable you are to pain instigated in the relationship. Have you ever hurt as much as you do when your spouse disappoints or betrays you? Probably not. Marriage is the relationship we are the most vulnerable in.

When you are in pain produced by your spouse, lean into God's guidance and wisdom. Pursue His heart through prayer and fasting. Make your way from pain to forgiveness and acceptance. Allow God to heal your heart and restore your vision and passion for your marriage. God has the answers to your dilemma.

You may not receive answers to every cross you bear. Trust God with the solutions to every situation you feel overwhelmed by. Trust Him to order your steps into peace and don't take a step without confirmation that it is a step that comes with God's blessing.

Pursue forgiveness. Pursue your marriage. Pursue your spouse. Pursue wholeness in your marriage. Pursue passion for the love of your life. You will never have what you do not pursue. Decide today what you want in your marriage and pursue it.

Marriage is an awesome opportunity for God's love to shine into our lives. Use tones and words to build a protective shell that shields your marriage from unnecessary conflict. Allow God's love to reflect in your attitude and words. Allow His heart to affect your heart and move you to be more willing to forgive.

The real goal of marriage should be to shine God's love through your relationship. Your witness to others is often displayed in the health of your marriage. Others will watch your love for your spouse succumb to pressure in your life, or resolve to be resilient and victorious.

Think about the light your marriage can be by overcoming the obstacles you two face, and being willing to persevere. Your marriage can become a beacon of hope for other couples in distress. Think about the testimony of couples who not only survive the storms of life, but thrive through their difficulties to find solace in their marriage relationship. It pleases God when couples persevere and find joy in friendship and marriage with their spouse. Marriage was created to provide safety, security, love and joy. Pursue God's plan for marriage, and love will always win!

You have a beautiful opportunity to love your spouse well. You have the opportunity to speak life into your spouse, forgive them, care for their heart, nurture their dreams, and believe in them. Pain, disappointment, and stress divide relationships and cause you to be distracted by feelings that overwhelm you and cause confusion in your heart.

Love wins when you decide to love your spouse despite your pain. Love wins when you decide that the welfare of the marriage is more important than your feelings, which are important, but only temporary.

Live fully, love infinitely, give generously, forgive frequently, and you will live a blessed life. Marriage is both beautiful and hard at the same time. The best part is we do not have to do it alone. The Author of your lives and the universe is rooting for you and cheering you on. He believes in your marriage and will give you strength to overcome any pain, loss, or illness you face in life. On your journey, I pray you find an unexplainable peace and joy that comes only from our Redeemer.

Love is more powerful than pain. Love always wins!

*God always allows us to feel the frailty of human love
so we'll appreciate the strength of His.*
C.S. Lewis

REFERENCES

Wooding, D. (2016). The porn phenomenon: A comprehensive new survey on Americans, the church, and pornography. *Good News Today.* http://thegoodnewstoday.org/

Cline, V.B., (1984). Obscenity—How it affects us, how we can deal with it. *The Church of Jesus Christ of Latter Day Saints.* https://www.lds.org/ensign/1984/04

Fagan, P.F., (2009). The effects of pornography on individuals, marriage, family and community. *MARRI Research Synthesis.* http://downloads.frc.org/EF/EF12D43.pdf

Gottman, John (1999). *The Seven Principles for Making Marriage Work.* New York, Crown Publishers.

Gottman, John (February 24, 2017). Lecture at Gottman Training Seminar Opryland Hotel Nashville, TN.

The Holy Bible. New International Version. (1984). Grand Rapids: Zondervan Publishing House.

Layden, M.A., Voon, V., Thomas, B. (July 14, 2015). *U.S. Capitol Symposium: Sexual Obesity: Research on the Public Health Crisis of Pornography.* Lecture at Pornography: A Public Health Crisis.

Malcolm, M., & Naugal, G., (2014). Are pornography and marriage substitutes for young men? *Institute of the Study of Labor.*

Murray, S. L., Bellavia, G. M., & Rose, P. (2003). Once hurt, twice hurtful: How perceived regard regulates daily marital interactions. *Journal of Personality and Social Psychology, 84*(1), 126.

Voon V, Mole TB, Banca P, Porter L, Morris L, Mitchell S, et al. (2014). Neural correlates of sexual cue reactivity in individuals with and without compulsive sexual behaviours. *PLoS ONE 9*(7): e102419.

About the Author

Beverly McManus

Beverly Cohron McManus is a Licensed Professional Counselor with a Mental Health Service Provider designation. She has a thriving private practice in Franklin, Tennessee with over 20 years of counseling experience.

Beverly believes we shape the future by our attitudes and beliefs. She helps clients find healing by shifting their mindset concerning hurts, traumas, and past experiences. She also focuses her practice on creating healthier relationships, thereby improving her clients' overall wellbeing—as research indicates unhealthy relationships can cause both emotional and physical stress.

She graduated from Tennessee State University with a Master's degree in Psychology, and earned a Doctorate in Counseling Education. As a part of her professional services, she provides supervision to counselor interns.

Beverly has been happily married to Kevin for over 18 years. She is Mom to a spunky redhead preteen, Kyle. She and her family are all involved in ministry at their local church. Beverly also speaks nationally at women's events and marriage conferences.

www.BeverlyMcManus.com

Book Sponsor

Representing most major brands of professional audio, video, and multimedia equipment, we are focused and committed to the house of worship systems integrations industry.

Our designs involve the coordination of architectural and theatrical lighting, projection screens, projection equipment, cameras, video support, audio equipment and support, acoustic treatment solutions, and training!

NT is more than an equipment vendor and systems integrator, we have a heart for worship with the experience and knowledge to analyze, evaluate and recommend with confidence, the perfect solution to your audio, video, lighting and multimedia needs.

Your initial consultation is free!

Please allow us an opportunity to be of service to your ministry.

Kevin T. McManus, President
Nashville Teleproductions, Inc.
1-800-883-1772
615-293-5728 mobile
www.nashvilleteleproductions.com

Our Written Lives
book publishing services
www.OurWrittenLives.com

www.ingramcontent.com/pod-product-compliance
Lightning Source LLC
Chambersburg PA
CBHW070103120526
44588CB00034B/2072